ALEXANDER HAMILTON

America's Bold Lion

JOHN ROSENBURG

Twenty-First Century Books
Brookfield, Connecticut

*To Ursula, Hans, and Andrea Rusch—
in appreciation for years of generosity
and support. JR*

Published by Twenty-First Century Books
A Division of The Millbrook Press, Inc.
2 Old New Milford Road
Brookfield, Connecticut 06804
www.millbrookpress.com

Library of Congress Cataloging-in-Publication Data
Rosenburg, John M.
Alexander Hamilton : America's bold lion / John Rosenburg.
p. cm.
Includes bibliographical references and index.
Summary: A biography of Alexander Hamilton, the first Secretary of the
Treasury of the United States, discussing his accomplishments as well as the
controversy and scandal that marked his career.
ISBN 0-7613-1617-5 (lib. bdg.)
1. Hamilton, Alexander, 1757–1804—Juvenile literature.
2. Statesmen—United States—Biography—Juvenile literature.
3. United States—Politics and government—1783–1809—Juvenile
literature. [1. Hamilton, Alexander, 1757–1804. 2. Statesmen.]
I. Title.
E302.6.H2 R67 2000
973.4'092—dc21 [B] 99-057292

Cover photographs courtesy of The Granger Collection, New York,
and North Wind Picture Archives

Photographs courtesy of The Bank of New York Archives: p. 4; The Granger
Collection, New York: pp. 17, 181; Museum of the City of New York: Gift of
Mrs. Alexander Hamilton and General Pierpont Morgan Hamilton, 71.31.5):
p. 25; The Monmouth County Historical Association, Freehold, New Jersey:
Gift of the Descendants of David Leavitt, 1937: p. 53; National Archives: p.
77; Stock Montage: p. 88; The New York Public Library: pp. 95 (Astor, Lenox
and Tilden Foundation, Stokes Collection), 175 (Wallach Division of Arts,
Prints, Photographs); Corbis-Bettmann: pp. 114, 171; National Portrait
Gallery, Smithsonian Institution/Art Resource, NY: pp. 123, 127; North Wind
Picture Archives: p. 134; Donaldson, Lufkin & Jenrette Collection of
Americana: p. 143; © Collection of The New-York Historical Society: p. 185

ALEXANDER HAMILTON

Alexander Hamilton

∽ Prologue ∽

When Alexander Hamilton was born, his future appeared to be anything but promising. His life, in fact, seemed headed for disaster.

Hamilton's mother was born in the West Indies as Rachel Faucett. When she was sixteen, Rachel married John Michael Lavien, a much older man, who was a failure in business but something of a dandy.

Some time after Rachel gave birth to Peter Lavien, their only child, John accused Rachel of "adultery with at least two men." Convicted of this serious crime, she was jailed in a fort on St. Croix.

When John Lavien was satisfied that Rachel had learned a lesson about what he called her "unholy way of life," he had her released from prison, convinced she would rejoin him.

But to Lavien's surprise and anger, Rachel ran away to the island of St. Kitts. Soon afterward, she moved in with a man named James Hamilton. They never married, but Rachel took his name.

James Hamilton was born in Scotland in about 1718, the fourth son of a rich and prominent family. He was raised in the family castle, called The Grange. When he grew up, he drifted to the West Indies and seemed never to hold a steady job.

Rachel and James Hamilton had two sons. The oldest was also named James. Alexander was the second son. He was born (according to his own statement) on January 11, 1757, on the tiny British island of Nevis, which made him a British subject.

In 1765, James Hamilton, Rachel, and their two sons went to St. Croix to live. A year later James Hamilton moved back to Nevis—alone.

With help from her relatives, Rachel opened a small store beneath a tiny apartment in Christiansted. But when Alexander was thirteen, Rachel died of a tropical fever, leaving behind several slaves, a few spoons and dishes, four dresses, a sun hat, a pair of sugar tongs, a few chests, and one bed, a clear indication that her sons slept on the floor of their apartment.

Six months after Rachel's death, her then-divorced husband, John Lavien, laid claim to her meager estate. He did so, he told the court, because the Hamilton brothers had been born in "whoredom" and his son, Peter, was the legitimate heir. The court agreed.

The court also appointed a cousin as guardian for the Hamilton boys. A year later, despondent over the death of his wife, the cousin committed suicide.

While young James Hamilton apprenticed to a carpenter following his mother's death, Alexander became a clerk in Nicholas Cruger's import-export company. It was then that Alexander's career began to take shape. It was a stormy, meteoric career that ended tragically.

Even so, Alexander Hamilton became one of America's most important Founding Fathers.

This is his story.

Part I

Early on a balmy fall day in 1771, William Newton, captain of the *Thunderbolt*, readied his newly built sloop for its maiden voyage. As the vessel bobbed restlessly against the lines holding it to a rotting pier in the crowded harbor of Christiansted on St. Croix, a messenger rushed up the gangplank and handed the captain his sailing orders.

The orders were signed by a clerk who assured Newton he was acting on behalf of the *Thunderbolt*'s absent owner, Nicholas Cruger.

In polite but firm language, Captain Newton was told he must leave the West Indies island that same day and "proceed immediately to Curacao." There, the clerk instructed, Newton should buy the best mules he could find, load as many as he could on *Thunderbolt*, and rush them back to St. Croix in time for the sugar harvest.

"Remember," the orders went on, "you are to make three trips this season and unless you are very diligent, you will be too late as our crops will be early in."

A few months later, the same clerk made a report to Cruger, who had gone to New York for health and business reasons. The *Thunderbolt*, the clerk said, had not only arrived late in St. Croix, but carried the "worse parcel of mules" he had ever seen. He wrote:

> She took in at first 48 & lost 7 on passage. I sent all that were able to walk to pasture, in number 33. The other 8 could hardly stand for 2 minutes together and in spite of the greatest care 4 of them are now in Limbo. The Surviving 4 I think are out of danger and shall likewise be shortly sent to pasture.
>
> I refused two great offers made me upon the first landing, to wit 7 pence a head for the aforementioned invalids . . .

By fattening the mules up, the clerk said proudly, he expected to get a hundred pounds a head.

When Captain Newton was again ready to sail, he received new orders from the clerk.

"I trust I may rely on you to perform your part with all possible diligence and dispatch," the orders read. "Reflect continually on the unfortunate voyage you have just made and endeavor to make up for the loss therefrom accruing to your owners. . . . This is all I think needful to say, so I wish you good passage."

The efficient and enterprising clerk who wrote those stern letters was fourteen-year-old Alexander Hamilton.

Although small for his age, young Hamilton loomed large in the minds of the little colony of whites living on St. Croix.

He worked hard at Cruger's and was very attentive to business details. His diligence, efficiency, respectful attention, and, most of all, his intelligence, impressed a wide range of people.

One of those who admired and befriended Hamilton was the Reverend Hugh Knox, a brilliant, though unconventional, Presbyterian minister.

Hamilton realized this was an important relationship for several reasons and eagerly cultivated it. Knox, for example, had a large library and introduced Hamilton to the world of books—books about religion, mathematics, chemistry, and philosophy.

Knox also encouraged Hamilton to write. Before long, poems written by Hamilton began to appear in the local gazette, drawing considerable attention.

It was a story about a hurricane, however, that prompted Knox, Nicholas Cruger, and others to do what civic-minded people often did in those days: pool their resources to send poor but promising young people to college.

Nicholas Cruger's, where Hamilton clerked, was on this street in Christiansted, St. Croix.

The story was part of a letter Hamilton had written in August 1772 to the father who had abandoned him. When Hamilton showed it to Reverend Knox, the minister was so impressed he gave it to the local newspaper. Hamilton wrote:

> It began about dusk, at North, and raged very violently till ten o'clock. Then ensued a sudden and expected interval which lasted about an hour. Meanwhile the wind was shifting round to the South West point, from whence it returned with redoubled fury and continued so till three o'clock in the morning. Good God! What horror and destruction—its impossible for me to describe it—or you to form any idea of it.
>
> It seemed as if a total dissolution of nature was taking place. The roaring of the sea and wind—fiery meteors flying about in the air—the prodigious glare of almost perpetual lightning—the crash of falling houses—and the ear-piercing shrieks of the distressed, were sufficient to strike astonishment in angels . . .

Hamilton was fifteen when he wrote this report. Years later, someone said the hurricane he so vividly described "blew him into history." In a way it did, for soon afterward, thanks to his friends, he was aboard *Thunderbolt* bound for school in America, arriving there soon after his sixteenth birthday.

⌒⌒

Since Hamilton had no formal education, his patrons arranged for his enrollment in an excellent Presbyterian preparatory school located in rural Elizabethtown, New Jersey.

Eager to advance as quickly as possible, Hamilton plunged into his studies of math, languages, and speech. Less than a year later, armed with a record of excellent grades, he went to New York for an interview with Dr. Myles Cooper, president of Kings College (now known as Columbia University).

Cooper was curious: Why didn't Hamilton go on to the College of New Jersey (now Princeton University), the path usually followed by the graduates of Elizabethtown?

Because, Hamilton replied, President John Witherspoon of the College of New Jersey insisted that he enroll as a regular four-year student. That was too slow for Hamilton. He wanted to receive private lessons so he could advance more quickly.

After considerable discussion, Cooper agreed to accept Hamilton, but warned that if he joined the school's twenty other students he must abide by the following rules:

- Academic dress at all times
- Attendance at all classes, meals, and prayers
- No dozing over books

- No climbing over the school gates after they were closed

- Violations meant fines

On September 20, 1774, Professor Robert Harpur, one of three teachers at Kings College, noted that Hamilton ". . . entered with me this day to study mathematics at three pounds, four shillings a quarter."

Starting in the mid-1700s the British government tried for ten years to collect a series of taxes from its colonies in North America to pay European war debts.

Many colonists thought the taxes were unfair and complained loudly. Others, calling themselves the Sons of Liberty, rioted.

To enforce collection of taxes and put down disturbances, British troops crossed the Atlantic to Boston. The violence and protests spread and escalated rapidly.

The colonists were not all of one mind, however. Some, who became known as Tories, supported the British Crown. Others, calling themselves Patriots, took the opposite view. Like students and others everywhere, Hamilton and his college friends were caught up in the controversy.

In the spring of 1774, Great Britain cracked down on Boston for the illegal act of dumping a shipment of tea into Boston harbor. The port was closed. More British troops arrived in the city and the royal government moved to Salem, Massachusetts.

The large building at the center of this view of the
northern outskirts of New York City is King's
College (now Columbia University). This
engraving dates from 1768, six years before
Hamilton enrolled at the college.

These and other drastic steps prompted the colonies to send delegates to a Continental Congress in Philadelphia "to concert a general and uniform plan for the defense and preservation of our common rights..."

The "uniform plan" had sharp teeth: It barred imports from England as well as exports to the homeland. Many were alarmed and angered by this drastic step, especially a New York Tory writer who signed himself as "A W. (Westchester) Farmer."

In an article titled "Free Thoughts on the Proceedings of the Continental Congress," he called those who attended the Congress "a parcel of upstart, lawless committeemen" who "basely betrayed the interests of the colonies." The Continental Congress, the writer added, hoped to subject the colonists to "abject slavery."

"Can men defend rights who act in open defiance of the law?" he asked.

Three weeks later, "A Friend to America" answered the Westchester farmer with a thirty-five-page pamphlet that included this scathing charge:

> They (the Tories) endeavor to persuade us that the absolute sovereignty of Parliament does not imply our absolute slavery; that it is a Christian duty to submit to be plundered of all we have, merely because some of our fellow subjects are wicked enough to require it of us; that slavery, so far from being a

great evil is a blessing; and even,
that our contest with Britain is
founded entirely upon the petty
duty of three pence per pound on
East India tea; whereas the whole
world knows it is built upon this
interesting question: whether the
inhabitants of Great Britain have a
right to dispose of the lives and
properties of the inhabitants of
America?

The "Friend to America" was seventeen-year-old
Alexander Hamilton. And while this was his first
political essay, it was far from his last.

∞

Six months after Hamilton's eighteenth birthday,
a second Continental Congress, provoked by
bloody battles between British troops and Patriots
in Massachusetts and elsewhere, agreed to establish a "Grand American Army" and set up a
Colonial civil government.

While many still hoped to reason with King
George's ministers and bring about a reconciliation, others were defiant. In New York, Hamilton
and his friends at Kings College formed a military
unit under the command of Captain Thomas
Fleming, a former officer of the British army.
Every day after classes, Hamilton and his little
group, armed with muskets, drilled among the
gravestones of a churchyard under Fleming's
watchful eye. Hamilton's "uniform" consisted of
a small round hat and a short green coat with a

star pinned to the chest area. The hat bore the words "Liberty or Death"; the star was inscribed "God and our Right."

On June 25, 1775, as Hamilton watched a parade of the local militia, his eyes were drawn to a tall, powerful-looking man who was wearing a buff and blue uniform and riding a big bay horse. This man would soon have a profound effect on Hamilton's life. His name was George Washington.

~

Even though the war in Massachusetts remained a stalemate through 1775, the Provincial Congress in New York City realized that, sooner or later, the British would attempt to establish a base of operations at the mouth of the Hudson River.

And when Commander in Chief Washington sent his second in command, Charles Lee, to New York to bolster its defenses, local authorities made a strong effort at recruitment.

A lieutenant was commissioned to establish an artillery company. For a time, the lieutenant was stymied; he could find no one qualified to act as captain and drill the company when it was formed.

When Hamilton learned of this situation, he immediately volunteered for the post. Did he have the background in mathematics to qualify as an artillery officer, the lieutenant asked. Hamilton said he believed he did.

Although skeptical, the recruiting officer told Hamilton that if he passed the required examination he would be accepted. That was all the encouragement Hamilton needed. He quickly located the appropriate army manuals and stepped up his studies with Professor Harpur.

Before long, he passed the exam, gave up his studies, and became, at nineteen, New York's top artillery officer.

∽∽

Hamilton's first muster in "The Fields" of lower Manhattan (now City Hall Park) early in 1776 was anything but promising.

Standing before him on that cold and windy day he saw a motley crew of fifty-five men of various ages and sizes. All were dressed in their own clothes. Only a handful had any military experience. And few were acquainted with the big, heavy guns they were now required to master.

In a meeting with his subordinate officers, Hamilton complained that the drummer couldn't keep a beat and the fifer sounded like "a screech owl."

Undeterred, Hamilton began correcting matters by ordering uniforms for his men—buckskin breeches, blue coats with buff lapels and brass buttons, matching shoes, and tricornered felt hats. The coats were lined with white, and white shoulder belts crossed the chest from shoulder to hips.

But Hamilton, who had developed a taste for elegant clothes, ordered a fancier uniform for himself: black boots, white breeches, a swallow-tailed blue coat, and a round cockaded hat with a chin strap.

And when drilling began, he replaced the drummer and fifer.

∞

Throughout his life, Alexander Hamilton tackled new projects, problems, and ventures with great enthusiasm and intensity, always seeking perfection.

His efforts with his artillery unit were typical. While he wanted a smart-looking team, he also labored diligently day after day to develop gunners who also would perform with distinction.

Late in April 1776, Hamilton was rewarded for his efforts. General Washington, who had recently arrived in New York with the Continental army, watched Hamilton and his corps perform during a typical Sunday muster. At the commander in chief's side stood Colonel Henry Knox, chief of artillery.

Washington and Knox were so impressed with the appearance and precision of Hamilton's gunners that they entrusted Hamilton with guarding the most important of more than a dozen artillery sites around New York City.

The sector, which Hamilton took over in June 1776, included the western end of the Grand Battery, a series of gun emplacements extending east to west across the southernmost tip of Manhattan Island.

Hamilton's group was barely in position when things began to happen. On June 29, for example, Sir William Howe, commander of the British army, showed up with his troops outside of New York harbor aboard a fleet of 110 battleships and transports. Over the next several days, Howe's troops went ashore on Staten Island, where they received a warm welcome from the predominately Tory population.

Ten days later, Washington had a momentous announcement read aloud to his troops by their commanders. It was the Declaration of Independence.

And at dawn on July 12, General Howe's brother, Admiral Richard "Black Dick" Howe, arrived aboard the flagship *Eagle*. The flagship was followed by another 150 vessels, each loaded with armament, supplies, redcoats (as the British soldiers were known), and Hessians (German mercenaries).

With the two fleets combined just across a few miles of water, the green American troops now faced the largest expeditionary force the world had ever seen.

At about noon, favored by a strong following wind and a flood tide, five British ships skimmed across the water toward Manhattan. Leading was *Phoenix*, a forty-four-gun battleship. It was followed by a frigate called *Rose* with twenty-eight guns, a schooner named *Tyral*, and two tenders.

The five ships sped toward the mouth of the Hudson. When they appeared to be within range, Hamilton gave the order to open fire. The guns roared, but the round fell short.

Reloading quickly and smoothly, the Americans fired again. But this time, several guns exploded! And when the smoke cleared,

Hamilton discovered that six of his men had been killed and four others wounded.

Unscathed, the enemy sailed to a safe anchorage upriver.

∞

Hamilton was grief-stricken by the deaths and wounding of his men. The explosion of his cannons also shook his confidence. Colonel Knox, however, was comforting. He insisted the gun explosions were accidental. He pointed out that Hamilton's artillery pieces were antiques and could blow apart with a normal charge of powder. He also said leftover sparks from the first volley may have ignited the second charge in some of the guns.

To Hamilton's relief, he was told that his guns and gunners would quickly be replaced, since a major attack could develop whenever the wind and tide favored the water-borne British.

Although there was no attack, a nervous and concerned Hamilton could see from his position on the tip of Manhattan that the enemy was continuing to build up its forces.

By mid-August, more than 40,000 professional enemy soldiers and sailors were positioned only a few miles away by water. Soon, Hamilton knew, they would try to conquer an ill-equipped force of amateurs half their number.

∞

At dawn on August 22, thousands of British and Hessian soldiers began to come ashore on Long

Looking smart and confident in his uniform, Captain Alexander Hamilton commanded an artillery unit that did its best with what few resources it had.

Island. The enemy's objective, it became evident, was to clear Brooklyn Heights of several thousand American troops in order to gain easy access to the East River and a good landing place for their troops.

To counter the move, Washington crossed the harbor to Brooklyn Heights with most of his army. Five days later, beginning early in the morning, a sustained rumble of gunfire rolled across the harbor, making it clear to Hamilton's tense gun crew at the Battery that a major battle had erupted somewhere on Long Island.

By mid-afternoon, it was over. The Americans, led in the field by Washington, had been cleverly outmaneuvered and suffered a severe defeat in their first open clash with the enemy.

Luckily, on the day of the battle a powerful northeast storm suddenly struck the area, creating headwinds that forced six British square-riggers to abort an attempt to get behind the Americans now huddled on Brooklyn Heights.

While the storm raged, however, the British slowly and methodically began siege operations. Howe's tactics seemed obvious; when the weather cleared, the British fleet would move into the East River and cut off Washington's only escape route. And after a period of "softening up," Howe's troops would storm the Heights, trying, in one blow, to end the war.

Overnight on August 29, however, Washington, in one of the most remarkable achievements in military history, secretly moved his army of 12,000 men to Manhattan without incident. The withdrawal marked the beginning of a long and painful retreat for the Americans—and with it, an abrupt change in Alexander Hamilton's life as a soldier.

∞

In mid-September, Hamilton and his gunners were forced to flee northward with other Patriot units when the enemy's combined land and naval command established a beachhead on Manhattan's eastern shore.

Within a month, General Howe had easily pushed the Americans out of New York City and established the town as his main base of operations. He then launched a campaign to destroy Washington's army and capture Philadelphia, the capital of colonial America.

The British began by driving the main Patriot army out of New York and across the Hudson River to New Jersey. Howe then chased the Americans steadily southward across the New Jersey plains. There was a brief delay at the Raritan River when Hamilton's two guns, hidden in a wood on high ground, helped destroy a bridge that would have allowed the British to cross the river and close in on the outnumbered and outgunned Americans.

Farther south, the enemy was again halted, this time at the shores of the broad Delaware River. When Hamilton and the rest of the Americans crossed to Pennsylvania, they took every available boat with them.

On December 13, with winter coming on, Howe suddenly changed tactics. He returned his main force to the comfort of New York, leaving garrisons at key locations in south Jersey, including Princeton, Bordentown, Brunswick, and Trenton. It was a move he would regret.

∞

Soon after the harrowing escape from the pursuing troops of Howe's army, Hamilton fell ill. This was a serious matter since it was bitterly cold and, like the rest of the army, Hamilton's unit was camped on the ice-covered shores of the Delaware River without shelter and with very little food.

But Hamilton was lucky. Henry Knox insisted on having the young captain carried to a small farmhouse that served as his headquarters. While Knox and his staff occupied the east wing of the house, Hamilton was put in a small back room where he could be fed and kept warm and dry.

At about noon on December 23, Knox squeezed his bulky body through the door of Hamilton's room and approached the bed. Obviously, he wanted to know how Hamilton was feeling. Better, his young captain answered weakly.

In the course of the conversation, Knox mentioned that the army would be leaving in the morning. Hamilton, he said, should remain behind until he was fully recovered.

But when the army broke camp at three the next afternoon—Christmas Eve—Hamilton was in uniform and clinging weakly to the back of a horse at the head of his unit; the last group in a long line of men, animals, and equipment to cross the Delaware.

Early on Christmas Day, the Americans virtually surrounded a large force of Hessians manning the garrison at Trenton. After a two-hour battle, during which Hamilton's gunners played a large part, the enemy surrendered.

Among the enemy casualties were twenty-five to thirty dead and many wounded. In addition, almost a thousand soldiers and officers were captured, along with a huge supply of arms and ammunition.

At a council of war held about noon, Washington, for a variety of reasons, decided to take his weary troops back to Pennsylvania.

Although still quite ill, Hamilton was with the army eight days later when it again crossed the Delaware, this time to set up camp below Trenton on the far side of Assunpink Creek.

General Lord Cornwallis, who had pursued Washington across New Jersey, promptly rushed a large body of troops to the area from Princeton the same day.

When Cornwallis tried to cross the bridge at Assunpink, however, his troops were forced back repeatedly by brisk artillery fire, part of it directed by Hamilton.

As it grew dark, Cornwallis suddenly broke off the fight. He was sure he could whip the Americans in the morning.

But when the sun rose, the Americans were gone. They had slipped around Cornwallis's left flank while he and his men slept. And by daylight, they were well on their way to Princeton.

The Americans were not yet out of danger, however. On a roughly parallel road, two British regiments were rushing to help Cornwallis. At about eight o'clock that morning, January 3, 1777, the two forces—one moving south, the other north—discovered each other. A pitched battle soon erupted in an orchard and adjoining fields. After a heavy exchange of gunfire, the outnumbered redcoats broke ranks and fled.

Moving quickly to the town of Princeton, the Americans discovered that enemy soldiers were holed up in Nassau Hall, a large stone building on the tiny campus of the College of New Jersey.

When Washington told an aide to bring up the artillery, the order was passed to Hamilton. Soon, Hamilton had two guns loaded and trained on the target. At a nod from Washington, Hamilton's crew opened fire. The redcoats inside Nassau Hall hurriedly exited the building and surrendered.

Washington, knowing that Cornwallis would soon be after him, quickly moved his army north to winter quarters at Morristown, New Jersey. But Hamilton was no longer with him. Still ill, he made his way to Philadelphia, where he was taken in by friends.

Not long afterward, the British withdrew from most of New Jersey to winter in the New York City area. This gave General Washington time to attend to a host of important administrative matters, one of which was to find an additional assistant, or aide-de-camp.

Washington told friends he was looking for a man who had good sense, a good disposition, was educated, and had an even temper.

In a typical letter, Washington said, "As to military knowledge, I do not expect to find gentlemen much skilled at it. If they can write a good letter, write quick, are methodical and diligent, it is all I expect to find in my aides."

Obviously, someone saw these qualities in Hamilton and recommended him. For on January 25, 1777, he read this notice in the Philadelphia *Evening Post*: "Captain Alexander Hamilton, by applying to the printer of this paper, may hear of something to his advantage."

On March 1, having recovered his health, Hamilton joined Washington's headquarters staff at Morristown as the new aide-de-camp.

Part II

Washington's office and living quarters in Morristown were in Freeman's Tavern, a small building located in the center of the village. Hamilton and the other aides also lived in the tavern, where they slept two to a bed in a room filled with beds.

Hamilton was the youngest of several aides; Colonel Robert Harrison was the oldest at age thirty-two. The brash Hamilton was warmly welcomed to the group. While Washington addressed him formally as "Colonel," the others at headquarters almost immediately called him "Ham," or "Hammy." Harrison dubbed him "the Little Lion."

But there was more than the camaraderie of the headquarters staff that appealed to Hamilton. For example, as an aide to Washington he could become acquainted, directly or indirectly, with the nation's top military and political leaders and, to some degree, contribute to the political and military decisions made by the commander in chief.

Hamilton's new job also allowed him to view the nation's struggle for independence from the highest possible vantage point, an advantage that would shape his future political thinking.

∽

Never shy about expressing his opinion, Alexander Hamilton had been writing to several leading New York Patriots about a variety of subjects ever since 1775, when he plunged into the published debate with the "Westchester Farmer."

Now, as the only officer from New York at headquarters, the provincial government of his home state asked to be kept informed of what was going on. Hamilton was happy to oblige.

As soon as he joined Washington's staff in March 1777, he wrote New York's Committee of Correspondence, saying:

> The present time is so unfruitful of
> events that it affords no intelligence
> worthy of your notice. As to trans-
> actions of a military nature, I can
> only say that the British Army con-
> tinues to decrease by the daily loss
> of prisoners and deserters taken at
> and coming into different posts,
> which is a striking symptom that
> the situation of affairs with the

enemy is not so favorable as it might be; for when an army is in good humor, and its affairs prosperous, desertion is a disease that seldom prevails in it.

In another note he said, "It is my opinion that the enemy will make no grand movement before the beginning of May; and perhaps not by then."

Early that summer, when General Howe's numerically superior force failed to lure Washington into battle on the plains of New Jersey where the terrain favored the enemy, Hamilton gave this explanation to his New York correspondents: "The liberties of America are an infinite stake. We should not play a desperate game for it or put it upon the issue of a single cast of the dice. The loss of one general engagement may effectually ruin us."

Hamilton also took it upon himself to comment on the framing of a new state constitution for New York. In addition, he blithely contacted John Jay and other New York delegates to Congress to give them advice about civil matters.

This was brash indeed. But Hamilton's arguments were often sound and always brilliantly expressed. As a result, he began to get a foothold in the New York political arena, which he would one day dominate.

෴

Three weeks passed before Hamilton could tell his New York correspondents that it now was certain the British commander in chief meant to capture Philadelphia and bring an end to the war for independence.

When Howe first entered the approaches to the Delaware River, Hamilton wrote, his spies warned that it was too risky to try and breach the Patriot defenses in the Delaware with square-rigged ships.

As a result, the enemy sailed south and rounded Virginia's Cape Charles into Chesapeake Bay, finally landing at Head of Elk (now Elkton), Maryland.

On September 1, Hamilton wrote again, saying, "The enemy will have Philadelphia if they dare make a bold push for it, unless we fight them a pretty general action. I opine we ought to do it, and that we shall beat them soundly if we do.

"I would not only fight them," he added boldly, "but I would attack them; for I hold it an established maxim that there is three to one in favor of the party attacking."

But Washington had a different plan.

The 40-mile (64-kilometer) stretch of land between Head of Elk and Philadelphia was open and fairly flat.

As Washington, Hamilton, and others studied skimpy maps and often-contradictory intelligence reports, it became obvious that Brandywine Creek was the best place to block the enemy's march on Philadelphia.

By September 10, Washington had his army of 11,000 in position along the east bank of the Brandywine with the bulk of his troops centered at Chad's Ford, one of many fords located along the slow-moving stream.

That night, General Howe's army of 5,000 Germans and 7,500 British camped only 5 miles (8 kilometers) away, in and around the village of Kennett Square.

Late in the afternoon of the next day, due to faulty intelligence, a massive enemy force made a surprise appearance behind the Americans' right flank.

Washington immediately left his post at the center of the American line and galloped toward the battle that had erupted on the right. Following closely behind were his aides, including Hamilton and the Marquis de Lafayette, a newcomer who had only recently arrived from France and joined Washington as a volunteer.

As they tried to rally the troops in this sector, some 5,000 enemy soldiers pushed across the Brandywine at Chad's Ford, forcing the weaker American left to splinter and fall back.

Within the next hour, Washington's army was in full retreat and on the road to Chester, Pennsylvania. Fortunately, the British main army was exhausted by the grueling 17-mile (27-kilometer) march that took it around the American right flank and were unable to follow, camping for the night.

Two weeks later, after outmaneuvering the Americans in the countryside, Howe marched his troops into Philadelphia without a shot being fired.

But despite the defeat at Brandywine, Hamilton wrote his friends in New York, the war wasn't over.

By late September, General Howe had the main body of his troops in Germantown, a hamlet 5 miles northwest of Philadelphia near the bank of the Schuylkill River.

The Americans were soon encamped 25 miles (40 kilometers) beyond Germantown at Potts Grove. Hoping for "another Trenton," Washington decided to launch a simultaneous attack against Howe's forces in Germantown from four different directions.

The jump-off was set for dawn, October 4. Unfortunately, a blinding fog enveloped Germantown when the battle erupted. As the Americans advanced, two brigades collided in the fog, mistook each other as the enemy, fired until they were out of ammunition, and ran to the rear in panic.

Hamilton, Washington, and other officers tried to rally the men. It was no use. The soldiers continued to flee the mysterious, unseen enemy. By ten o'clock, the battle was over.

Part of Hamilton's role as Washington's aide was to assemble and assess intelligence received at headquarters.

After the army moved west of Germantown to the village of Whitemarsh, he reported that Howe's army was still "vulnerable" and could be conquered.

Hamilton reasoned that if the Americans could continue to block the Delaware River,

Howe would be separated from his navy. And without the navy, his supplies would have to travel overland from Head of Elk, a 40-mile route difficult to protect.

But, Hamilton pointed out, to keep the British navy out of the Delaware and to retake Philadelphia, reinforcements would be needed. Hamilton then raised the obvious question: Where would reinforcements come from?

No one knew the answer. But suddenly and almost miraculously, Hamilton found a message from New York Governor George Clinton that he joyfully read aloud to Washington and his staff:

> Albany, N. Y., Oct 15, 1777:
> Last night at 8 o'clock the capitulation, whereby General Burgoyne and the whole (British) army surrendered themselves prisoners of war was signed . . .

Burgoyne, he said excitedly, had been defeated near Saratoga, New York, by General Horatio Gates on September 19.

That meant, Hamilton added, that Gates and his subordinate, General Putnam, could now send Washington enough men to keep Howe's army bottled up in Philadelphia!

Gates and Putnam, however, had other ideas.

∞

Horatio Gates was described by one writer as "a little, ruddy-faced Englishman peering through his thick spectacles." He also said Gates was "a snob of the first water" who had "unctuously pious ways about him." Others said Gates had "a repellent personality."

As second in command, Gates was obliged to immediately send Washington the official report on Burgoyne's capitulation and a copy of the surrender terms. But Gates sent his reports to Congress and left it to Congress to supply Washington with the details of his victory.

This amounted to insubordination. And the situation worsened when Gates and Putnam failed to send the reinforcements Washington repeatedly requested. Finally, at a council of war, a unanimous decision was reached: An officer fully authorized to act for the commander should be sent North immediately to confront the balky generals.

The officer chosen was twenty-year-old Alexander Hamilton.

Hamilton began the 300-mile (483-kilometer) journey from Whitemarsh, Pennsylvania, to Albany, New York, on October 31, accompanied by Caleb Gibbs, captain of the headquarters guard. In his saddlebags, Hamilton carried letters of authority written by Washington to both Gates and Putnam.

In two days of hard riding, Hamilton and Gibbs covered the first 150 miles, reaching the Hudson River at dark. After an overnight rest on the west bank of the Hudson, the two crossed to the east bank and by the end of the day rode into Putnam's camp.

When Hamilton met the round-faced, fifty-nine-year-old Israel Putnam, he was cordially received. But when he turned the conversation to reinforcements, Putnam kept insisting he preferred to hold on to his force so he could attack New York—an improbable plan without the aid of a navy.

Hamilton finally told Putnam he was to immediately send Washington two brigades of Continentals that Putnam had received from Gates; one under General Ebenezer Learned, the other under General Enoch Poor. Grudgingly, Putnam agreed.

Hamilton now hurried north to complete what he knew would be the more difficult part of this important mission.

Hamilton's first meeting with Gates took place at the pudgy general's headquarters in Albany, some 20 miles (32 kilometers) south of his victory over Burgoyne, clearly the most important of the war.

Unlike General Putnam, Gates was far from cordial. In fact, he was hostile, saying immediately that he didn't have much time to talk, that he knew why Hamilton had come, and that he could only spare one brigade—"Patterson's."

Hamilton, calm and polite, said he must give Washington a logical reason as to why Gates needed to keep two brigades (close to 10,000 men) when the nearest enemy was hundreds of miles away. But Gates was adamant. It was the Patterson brigade or none.

Realizing that further argument was useless, Hamilton broke off the discussion but said he would be back the next day.

As he strode unhappily across the campgrounds he ran into his old college roommate, Robert Troup. Troup, it turned out, was aide-de-camp to Gates.

Troup warned Hamilton that Gates was the "toast of New England and the army." He said letters of commendation were pouring in from the public every day. Often, he said, Gates read the letters to his staff.

One letter, in fact, was from one of Washington's own generals, Thomas Conway. Hamilton was stunned. He didn't think Conway knew Gates.

Troup also noted that many of the letters were critical of Washington. Some, he said, even hinted at what, for Hamilton, was unthinkable—that Gates should replace Washington.

After leaving Troup, Hamilton hurried to his quarters and wrote a letter to Washington telling him of his encounter with Gates.

"I arrived here yesterday at noon," he wrote, "and waited upon General Gates immediately . . . but was sorry to find his ideas did not correspond with yours for drawing off the number of troops you directed."

He then warned that Gates's victory over Burgoyne had won for Gates "the entire confidence of the Eastern states" and had given him "influence and interest elsewhere."

Hamilton said he wouldn't press Gates for more than one brigade and hoped that he wasn't making a mistake. But Hamilton discovered that the Patterson brigade Gates offered to send Washington was far below normal strength.

Angered by what appeared to be a deliberate deception, Hamilton decided to confront Gates. But first he put his thoughts on paper. In a letter to Gates dated November 4, he said, "By inquiry I have learned that General Patterson's brigade, which is the one you propose to send, is by far the weakest of the three now here and does not consist of more than six-hundred rank and file fit for duty [instead of one-thousand or more] . . ." He said that Gates should select another brigade "without loss of time."

Determined to have a showdown, Hamilton took the letter to Gates's headquarters. The general, aide-de-camp Troup told him, was in the field. Hamilton said he would wait.

When Gates arrived, Hamilton handed him the letter and said he hoped Gates would reconsider his position. After a heated discussion, Gates reluctantly added a second brigade to Patterson's and ordered the immediate departure of both.

Two days later, however, Hamilton's mission stalled again.

∞

"I am pained beyond expression to inform your Excellency that on my arrival I find everything has been neglected and deranged by General Putnam, and that the two brigades—Poor's and Learned's—still remain here."

44

So wrote Hamilton to Washington on November 10, 1777, on his arrival back at Putnam's camp with Caleb Gibbs. Putnam, Hamilton reported, was far to the south with a body of militia embarked on an expedition against New York.

Putnam, he added, had ignored the order to send reinforcements to Washington. "Everything," he said, "is sacrificed to the whim of taking New York."

Putnam's departure was not the only problem. The Poor and Learned brigades "would not march for want of money and necessities," he noted. As a result there had been a "high mutiny" among Poor's men that ended in tragedy. "A Captain killed a man, and was shot himself by the man's comrade," Hamilton said.

To get the troops moving, Hamilton, through Governor George Clinton, arranged for a loan of about $6,000 which, he told Washington, should keep the men "in good humor till they join you."

Hamilton also fired off a letter to Putnam, saying, "I now, sir, in the most explicit terms, by his Excellency's authority, give it as a positive order from him that all Continental troops under your command be immediately marched..."

Hamilton's orders were ignored and Washington never received any of the requested reinforcements. As a result, Howe's forces were able to open the Delaware River to the British navy, and Philadelphia remained in the hands of a numerically superior army.

Washington had no choice but to withdraw to a place called Valley Forge for the winter, where scores would die of starvation and exposure in extremely cold and snowy weather.

As for Hamilton, he became so ill that Gibbs thought the dauntless little captain was going to die. The two remained in Peekskill, New York, for two months.

The return journey took two weeks longer than the ride to Gates, ending at Washington's headquarters at dusk on January 12, 1778.

After a warm greeting by his colleagues, Hamilton learned that his worst fear might come true: Washington, the man he considered the army's best general, might be replaced as commander in chief by the untrustworthy Horatio Gates.

Support to remove Washington in favor of Gates collapsed, however. Then, in the spring, the world changed. France recognized the independence of the American states, became a powerful military ally, and, in effect, declared war against England.

Part III

British military plans to conquer George Washington's army and regain control of England's former colonies changed swiftly and dramatically when France signed a treaty of alliance with the Americans early in 1778.

The one-sided battle that pitted a mighty land and sea power against an upstart land-bound force of military misfits now became a global war between two of the world's largest and most powerful armies and navies.

In the spring of 1778, Sir William Howe was recalled to England and Sir Henry Clinton replaced him as commander in chief of the British forces. Then came word that the 10,000-man British army would be shifted from Philadelphia to its main base in the New York City area. With the French fleet expected in American waters any day, General Clinton decided to move overland to

New York, avoiding the risk of losing his troops at sea in a naval battle.

When word of the British intentions reached Valley Forge, George Washington's army, idle for almost eight months, sprang to life and began to shadow the enemy columns. At the right moment, Washington hoped to strike what might prove to be a fatal blow. The opportunity came sooner than expected.

By the start of the new campaign, Hamilton had had enough of paperwork. He did recognize that Washington gave him many interesting assignments that took him away from his desk. With a handful of men, for example, Hamilton had destroyed a flour mill to keep it out of enemy hands. He also negotiated a prisoner exchange and wrote a plan for reorganizing the army that was submitted to Congress.

But these diversions failed to satisfy Hamilton's restless spirit. He wanted action, wanted to be at the head of troops in the field.

On June 24, only six days after the army left Valley Forge, it appeared he would have his chance. By then the Americans had reached Hopewell, New Jersey, a position not far from the line of march the British had taken to reach New York.

After a hot debate during a council of war, a small body of troops was ordered to attack the enemy's left flank near Monmouth Court House while the main army made ready for a full-scale engagement.

Since Washington was to remain with the larger force, General Charles Lee, second in command, was offered the opportunity to lead the attack. Because he had argued against such a move during the council debate, Lee declined.

Washington then settled on Lafayette, the young French volunteer. Hamilton promptly asked to serve as aide to the Marquis. Washington granted his permission.

As Lafayette and Hamilton hurried through the night to organize their troops for an attack on the British left flank, however, they received a startling order from headquarters: Lee had changed his mind! He would take over. Lafayette was to go to Englishtown, a dejected Hamilton back to headquarters.

On his return to headquarters, Hamilton quickly reviewed the military situation for Washington and his generals.

His appraisal boiled down to this: Lee was in command of 5,000 to 6,000 men and twelve cannons only 6 miles (10 kilometers) from the tail end of the British column at Monmouth Court House. Washington, with another 7,000, was 3 miles (5 kilometers) east of Lee. Lee had twice been ordered to attack as soon as the British began to move northward.

Soon after delivering his report, Hamilton was ordered to scout the country between Lee and his advance corps for any sign of the enemy and report back to headquarters.

Hamilton quickly completed his scouting mission even though the day was excessively hot and muggy. He then took the road back to headquarters only to discover Washington coming toward him at the head of the main body of troops.

When the two met, Hamilton told the commander he had found no one between Lee's troops and Lee's advance force. He said he had told Lee he did see about a thousand enemy foot soldiers and cavalry preparing to attack and suggested a counterattack to turn the enemy to the left.

Lee agreed, according to Hamilton, and asked Hamilton to pass the order. After he did so, Hamilton hurried to advise Washington as to what had taken place.

Washington was puzzled. If Lee had launched the attack, he and Hamilton should be hearing musketry, a sure sign the two forces were engaged in combat. There was only silence.

Suddenly, however, the two heard several cannon shots. Then more silence. At that moment, a farmer trudged toward them along the dusty road, telling anyone who would listen that the Americans were retreating.

Washington and Hamilton were stunned. Soon they learned the awful truth: Coming directly toward them at the head of his troops was General Lee.

∽

When Washington came close to Lee, he flew into a rage and excoriated the general for disobeying orders. Lee lamely tried to explain his actions, but before he got very far, Hamilton interrupted.

Waving a dispatch he had just received, Hamilton shouted that the enemy was only fifteen minutes away and moving fast.

Washington promptly forgot about Lee and rushed Lee's troops to a wood on the left of the road behind a thick hedgerow and a protective swamp.

Shouting orders as they galloped their horses back and forth, Washington, Hamilton, and other officers soon had the weary men formed for battle with General Stirling on the left, General Anthony Wayne in the center, General Nathanael Greene to the right, and Lafayette in a backup position.

The enemy sparked the action with a charge of cavalry at the Patriot center. Showing the effects of their training by Baron von Steuben, a volunteer German drillmaster, the Americans held their fire until the redcoated riders were almost upon them, then let go with what seemed to be a single volley. Down went horses and men in a bloody heap. Those who survived that withering initial blast turned and fled.

Now, marching in an almost straight line, the British infantry moved slowly forward. Again, American muskets and artillery halted the enemy.

After failing to turn the American right and left flanks, the British slowly retreated. By nightfall, enemy troops were behind good protective cover. Washington then decided to rest his men and resume the attack in the morning. Under cover of darkness, however, Clinton's men slipped away.

*Pictured in the battle of Monmouth Court House,
General Washington is followed on horseback by
Lafayette and Hamilton.*

On June 29, the day after the battle, the heat and humidity were just as punishing as the day before. And since the British had a long lead, it was clear the Americans could not hope to catch them.

As the army moved northward, General Lee wrote Washington and asked for a formal court-martial so he could justify his actions before the battle. Washington didn't hesitate. Lee was placed under arrest and charged with disobeying orders, misbehavior before the enemy, and showing disrespect toward the commander in chief.

Lee was found guilty of all charges and suspended from duty for twelve months. His case then went to Congress for review.

⚭

Almost from the moment he was court-martialed, General Charles Lee tried to convince his friends in Congress and elsewhere that he was wrongfully charged and convicted for his behavior at Monmouth Court House.

In a newspaper article, in fact, he took credit for "the success" of the day and said Washington had ". . . scarcely any more to do than strip the dead . . ."

Lee also made sarcastic comments about the prosecution witnesses at the trial, including Hamilton and Baron von Steuben.

Feeling he had been insulted, von Steuben immediately challenged Lee to a duel with guns, a common gesture in those days. When Lee assured the German he had not meant to sully his character, von Steuben withdrew his challenge.

At army headquarters at Middlebrook (now Bound Brook), New Jersey, word circulated that Hamilton also planned to challenge Lee. When he heard this, Washington forbade Hamilton to do so. Unknown to Washington, however, Hamilton's close friend John Laurens challenged Lee for insulting Washington. Lee accepted.

Arrangements for the duel went forward rapidly. Hamilton would act as Laurens's second, or assistant; Major Evan Edwards as Lee's.

The duel took place 4 miles (6.5 kilometers) outside of Philadelphia at 3:30 P.M. on December 23. On a signal from Hamilton, Lee and Laurens immediately advanced toward each other. Suddenly, both men fired. No one went down. But as Laurens raised his second pistol, Lee cried out, "I'm hit!"

Laurens, Hamilton, and Edwards rushed toward Lee. As they approached, they could see a red stain spreading through Lee's clothes.

Lee insisted it was only a flesh wound. He wanted to continue. Laurens agreed. But Hamilton and Edwards said matters had gone far enough. The duel was over.

While this was Hamilton's first experience with duels, it wouldn't be his last. As for General Lee, Congress upheld his conviction and eventually dismissed him from the army.

There was one subject that was discussed endlessly at headquarters: manpower. Where could the army find new recruits to fill the ranks constantly depleted by desertion, disease, casualties, and expired enlistments? And since parts of the south had already been invaded by the enemy, how could the army regain control of the area without more men?

Early in 1779, Hamilton revealed that he and John Laurens had fashioned a plan for a new source of manpower: slaves.

With Washington's approval, Hamilton wrote to John Jay, an old New York friend, who was then president of Congress:

"Colonel Laurens, who will have the honor of delivering you this letter, is on his way to South Carolina, on a project which I think, in the present situation of affairs, is a very good one, and deserves every kind of support and encouragement," Hamilton told Jay.

Laurens's mission, he said, "is to raise two, three, or four battalions of Negroes (slaves)" with the assistance of South Carolina and "take those battalions into Continental pay" to fight the British.

"It appears to me," Hamilton told Jay, "that an expedient of this kind, in the present state of southern affairs, is the most rational that can be adopted, and promises very important advantages. Indeed, I hardly see how a sufficient force can be collected in that quarter without it; and the enemy's operations there are growing infinitely serious and formidable."

Hamilton was well acquainted with slavery since he was reared among slaves in Christiansted, where they outnumbered whites by three to one. Hamilton said he had "not the least doubt" that blacks would make "very excellent soldiers."

"I have frequently heard it objected to the schemes of embodying Negroes, that they are too stupid to make soldiers," he added. "This is so far from appearing to me a valid objection that I think their want of cultivation (for their natural faculties are probably as good as ours), joined to the habit of subordination which they acquire from a life of servitude will make them sooner to become soldiers than our white inhabitants."

Hamilton said he knew this proposal would be opposed because of "prejudice and self-interest."

"The contempt we have been taught to entertain for blacks, makes us fancy many things that are founded neither in reason nor experience," he went on.

He also realized, he said, that Southern plantation owners would be unwilling to part "with property of so valuable a kind" and would oppose it with "a thousand arguments . . ."

He said, however, that if the Americans didn't recruit the slaves, the British would. An essential part of the plan to prevent this, he said, was to give slaves "their freedom with their swords."

Then, more than eighty years before the Civil War, he raised an unheard of idea with these words about his suggested offer of freedom:

"This will secure their fidelity, animate their courage, and, I believe, will have a good influence on those who remain (in slavery) by opening the door to their emancipation. This circumstance, I confess, has no small weight in inducing me to wish the success of the project; for the dictates of humanity and true policy, equally interest me in favor of this unfortunate class of men . . ."

The proposal won the approval of Congress. But the southern states, reluctant to give up their major source of labor, and fearful that armed blacks might turn against their masters, did not go along.

By the spring of 1779, army headquarters was back in Morristown so Washington's command could keep a close eye on Sir Henry Clinton in New York.

Not long afterward, Hamilton made a somber report to Washington's staff, based on recent intelligence delivered to headquarters.

Clinton, Hamilton said, had put troops aboard ships in New York City and with swift strokes captured a small American-held fort on the west side of the Hudson River at Stony Point and another opposite on the east bank at Verplank's Point.

It was, all recognized, a smart and strategically important move; the two forts guarded a river crossing called Kings Ferry, the best communications link between the eastern and southern states.

There was now another danger: the possible loss of West Point, farther up the river. Although unfinished, West Point was America's most important military fortification because it had the potential of blocking the Hudson and preventing the enemy from cutting off New England and almost all of New York from the rest of the colonies.

Within hours of Clinton's bold move, the army left the Morristown area and marched for the Hudson. Surprisingly, however, Clinton made no attempt to take West Point. After stationing troops at the two forts that controlled King's Ferry, Clinton put the bulk of his army aboard ship and sailed back to his stronghold in New York.

A month later General Anthony Wayne met with Washington and Hamilton at a new head-quarters in New Windsor. When the meeting ended, Hamilton wrote a set of orders for Wayne: On July 15, he was to make a surprise nighttime attack on Stony Point.

Hamilton wanted to join Wayne, but Washington said no. The area was infested with spies and Washington wanted activities at head-quarters to appear normal.

At about 9 o'clock on the morning of July 15, a messenger galloped into camp and handed Hamilton a message from Wayne; the fort and garrison had been captured and, Wayne added, "our officers and men behaved like men who are determined to be free."

In minutes, Washington, Hamilton, and the other aides were on their horses and rushing toward Stony Point, hoping to cross the river and mount an attack on Verplank's Point. When the attempt failed, the Americans gave up Stony Point, which was soon retaken by the British.

Still, West Point seemed secure. Work on its fortifications continued, and the garrison was turned over to one of Washington's favorite combat generals: Benedict Arnold.

⚭

With the French navy having sailed in and out of American waters and Clinton reported to be ready to leave New York for a campaign in the south, Washington moved headquarters from the Hudson back to Morristown.

The winter of 1779–1780 was as bitter and difficult as that endured at Valley Forge two years earlier. For Hamilton, it was also frustrating; Washington kept turning him down for a post as a combat commander, saying he could not place him over officers with more seniority.

Then came a new development: Hamilton's friend John Laurens, a member of a prominent South Carolina family and son of a former president of Congress, had been offered an assignment in Paris as secretary to Benjamin Franklin, the American minister to France.

In a letter to Hamilton, Laurens said he had declined the appointment and recommended Hamilton. Laurens told Congress that Hamilton was equally qualified "in point of integrity—and much better in point of ability."

Congress was not impressed. Hamilton failed to get the appointment. Bitterly disappointed, he thought he knew why: He was a foreigner, he had been born out of wedlock, and he didn't have the support of important people.

"I am a stranger in the country," he wrote Laurens. "I have no property here and no connexions. If I have talents and integrity (as you say I have) these are justly deemed very spurious titles in these enlightened days, when unsupported by others more solid."

Hamilton also complained to Laurens that Washington had blocked his attempts to get a command in the South. "Arguments have been used to dissuade me from it, which, however little weight they may have had in my judgment, gave law to my feelings," he said. "I am chagrined and unhappy but I submit.

"In short, Laurens, I am disgusted with everything in this world but yourself and very few more honest fellows."

Suddenly, however, Hamilton's life brightened. He fell in love.

Her name was Elizabeth "Betsey" Schuyler. A pretty brunette with large, lively, dark eyes, she was the twenty-three-year-old daughter of General Philip Schuyler, one of the richest and most powerful political figures in New York State.

Betsey made the trip from her home in Albany to Morristown in February 1780 to visit her cousin, Sarah Livingston, daughter of one of Hamilton's early benefactors, New Jersey Governor William Livingston.

On Betsey's arrival, Hamilton invited Betsey and Sarah to one of the "dancing assemblies" held at regular intervals at an army storehouse.

Less than a month later, he wrote Betsey's sister, Margarita, whom he had never met. "I venture to tell you in confidence that by some odd contrivance or other, your sister has found the secret of interesting me in everything that concerns her," he said.

Two weeks later, he and Betsey announced their engagement. And when Betsey returned to Albany to prepare for the wedding, the smitten Hamilton wrote her, "I love you more and more every hour. The sweet softness and delicacy of your mind and manners, the elevation of your sentiments, the real goodness of your heart—its tenderness to me—the beauties of your face and person—your unpretending good sense and that innocent simplicity and frankness which pervade your actions, all these appear to me with increasing amiableness, and place you in my estimation above all the rest of your sex."

While three of Betsey's sisters had eloped, Betsey and Hamilton planned a formal ceremony that would take place in December 1780. And once married to Betsey Schuyler, Hamilton would reach the three important personal goals he felt he lacked when he had hoped to win the appointment as secretary to Benjamin Franklin: He would have "family," "social connection," and, eventually, "property."

Early in 1780, a small French fleet had arrived in Newport, Rhode Island, commanded by Comte de Rochambeau, with nearly 10,000 French troops aboard. For the first time, French soldiers appeared ready to take up arms on American soil to help the Patriots in their struggle for independence.

Unfortunately, a flotilla of British warships sailed into Newport waters a day later and effectively bottled up the French vessels.

In late September, however, Hamilton, Lafayette, and other aides suddenly learned they were to accompany Washington on a secret journey to Hartford, Connecticut, for a conference with the French.

"On our return," Hamilton wrote Betsey from Hartford, "the General hopes to stop at West Point, inspect the works and visit his friends the Arnolds. It should be a happy occasion."

It wasn't.

There was one officer in Washington's command that Hamilton admired above all others—Benedict Arnold. Although never in the field with Arnold, Hamilton was well acquainted with his record, which showed that Arnold was the best combat general in either the British or American armies.

Hamilton was also aware that Arnold had been repeatedly passed over for promotion in favor of officers with less experience and seniority, mainly because politicians often selected and promoted officers from their home states when openings occurred.

Arnold was powerfully built at 5 feet, 9 inches (175 centimeters) in height and had black hair, dark skin, a beaked nose, and icy gray eyes.

When a severe leg wound suffered during the battle of Saratoga prevented him from riding a horse, Arnold became commander of the army post in Philadelphia after the British left the city.

In April 1789, Arnold, then thirty-eight, married a pretty, vivacious girl from a prominent Philadelphia family named Margaret "Peggy" Shippen. She was nineteen.

Later, Arnold asked for and received appointment as commander of West Point, in charge of some 4,000 men and all the American forts in the Hudson Highlands.

The house he and Peggy lived in, and which served as his headquarters, was owned by a Tory named Beverly Robinson. It stood on a high bluff on the east bank of the Hudson, directly across from West Point.

As Washington's entourage approached the Robinson house on its return from Hartford, Washington asked Hamilton to ride ahead and tell the Arnolds he would like to have breakfast with them. He did this as a courtesy, since the Arnolds had no way of knowing just when Washington and his group would arrive.

Delighted with the chance to have a few moments alone with one of his heroes and his lovely wife, Hamilton galloped off.

When Hamilton arrived at the Robinson house, however, he was disappointed to learn that Arnold had just left to prepare a welcome for Washington. He was even more disappointed when he was told that Peggy Arnold was too ill to see anyone.

Hamilton conveyed all this to Washington when the commander and his other aides arrived for the much anticipated breakfast.

When breakfast had been consumed and Arnold failed to appear, Washington decided to cross to West Point to meet Arnold and inspect the works. An unhappy Hamilton remained behind to deal with a pile of paperwork.

Late that morning, Hamilton received a bundle of papers from a Colonel Jameson, who was stationed nearby on the east bank of the Hudson. Since it was marked "urgent and private," Hamilton set it aside.

When Washington returned at about three o'clock he immediately asked whether Arnold had returned. Hamilton said he had not seen or heard from Arnold. He then handed Washington the papers he received earlier from Colonel Jameson.

Since it was close to the dinner hour, Hamilton, Washington, and Lafayette went to their rooms to prepare for the evening meal. The rooms adjoined each other on the ground floor.

As Hamilton began to change his clothes, he heard a loud cry of anguish and rage. The voice was Washington's.

Alarmed, Hamilton called to Lafayette, hurried down the hall to Washington's room, and threw the door open.

"Arnold has betrayed us!" a shaken Washington exclaimed as Hamilton and Lafayette entered his room. The proof, he said, was in the papers sent him by Colonel Jameson.

Washington then explained that the papers contained all the information the enemy would need to launch a successful attack on West Point. The papers, he said grimly, were in Arnold's handwriting and had been found in the boots of a "John Anderson," who had been captured on the east bank of the Hudson by three Patriot militiamen. This "Anderson," Washington added, admitted that he was Major John Andre, adjutant general of the British army.

Turning to Hamilton, Washington gave the young colonel a crisp order: Get on a fast horse and catch Arnold before the traitor reaches the British lines!

The forts guarding Kings Ferry (Verplank's Point on the east bank and Stony Point on the west) were about 12 miles (19 kilometers) below West Point. They had been seized by the Americans when General Clinton chose to evacuate them and send a large body of his troops into the southern theater.

When Hamilton reached Verplank's Point, the agitated officer on duty confirmed that Arnold had passed several hours earlier. He told the officer he was going aboard the *Vulture* (a British ship anchored in the river) under a flag of truce to meet the captain on orders from General Washington.

Hamilton quickly wrote an explanatory note to Washington and the following message to General Greene, who was with the main army in New Jersey:

> Verplank's Point, September 25,
> 1780
>
> There has just unfolded at this
> place a scene of the blackest
> treason. Arnold has fled to the
> enemy—Andre, the British Adjutant
> General, is in our possession as a
> spy. His capture unraveled the
> mystery.
>
> West Point was to have been the
> sacrifice. All the dispositions have
> been made for this purpose, and 'tis
> possible, though not probable, we
> may still see the execution. The
> wind is fair (upriver). I came here in
> pursuit of Arnold, but was too late.
> I advise your putting the Army
> under marching orders and
> detaching a brigade immediately
> this way.

On his return to the Robinson house, Hamilton
found Lafayette waiting for him with astonishing
news: Peggy Arnold, Lafayette said, had lost her
mind.

Despite all the turmoil at headquarters, Hamilton
managed to write to Betsey, describing the major
events that were taking place during this dramatic
period in the war.

A few hours after he had left in pursuit of
Arnold, Hamilton wrote, Peggy screamed for
Washington. When he went to her room, he

found her hysterical. She screamed some more and accused the general of trying to kill her baby. He tried to soothe her, but it was no use.

The next day, Hamilton wrote Betsey, "I saw an amiable woman frantic with distress for the loss of a husband she tenderly loved—a traitor to his country and to his fame, a disgrace to his connections. It was the most affecting scene I was ever witness to. She for a considerable time entirely lost her senses."

"All the sweetness of beauty, all the loveliness of innocence, all the tenderness of a wife and the fondness of a mother showed themselves in her appearance and conduct," he added.

Hamilton said he believed Peggy knew nothing of Arnold's plans, and arrangements were made to send her and her child to her family in Philadelphia.

∽

Shortly after talking to Peggy Arnold, Hamilton paid a visit to Major Andre, who was being held under guard in a tavern in Tappan, New York, now Washington's temporary headquarters.

In the course of a long and cordial conversation, Hamilton raised several questions related to Andre's capture. Andre told Hamilton this story:

He left the *Vulture* and went ashore on the west bank of the Hudson in full uniform on the night of September 22. A meeting with Arnold behind the American lines lasted through the night. Early the next morning, without Arnold's knowledge, the American commander at Verplank's Point sent two pieces of artillery down the east bank and aimed them at the *Vulture*. The captain quickly moved his vessel downstream, making it impossible for Andre to return to the ship.

Arnold then talked Andre into changing into civilian clothes and convinced him he should cross the river at Kings Ferry, go down the east bank and back to the British lines. In case he was stopped, he could use a pass signed by Arnold made out to "John Anderson." All went well until Andre reached Tarrytown, where he was seized and searched by the three militiamen.

Hamilton knew the rest of the tale. Because he was in civilian clothes and carrying military secrets to the enemy, Andre was charged with being a spy by a military court, found guilty, and sentenced to death by hanging.

Andre insisted he was not a spy. And he resented being hanged like a common criminal. If he had to die, he told Hamilton, he should be shot while dressed in his full uniform.

As the story unfolded, Hamilton suddenly felt a wave of compassion for the prisoner. And because Andre was obviously a well-educated and brave soldier, Hamilton also came to admire him.

But there was something else. In piecing together information about Arnold's plot to deliver West Point to the enemy, which might have led to the capture of Washington, Hamilton concluded that Arnold planned a double betrayal. If his meeting with Andre on the west bank was discovered, he would blame all on Andre to save his own skin.

The prospect of this double betrayal convinced Hamilton to try and help the condemned Andre.

Without authority, Hamilton wrote a letter to Sir Henry Clinton suggesting that Andre's life could be saved if he were "released for General Arnold."

"Major Andre's character and situation seem to demand this of your justice and friendship," Hamilton wrote the British commander. "Arnold appears to have been the guilty author of the mischief; and ought more properly be the victim."

Hamilton also told Clinton there was "great reason" to believe Arnold planned "a double treachery, and had arranged the interview in such a manner, that if discovered . . . he might have it in his power to sacrifice Major Andre to his own safety."

But Hamilton's letter was too late. By the time it reached Clinton, Andre had already been executed.

In the fall of 1780, Alexander Hamilton, for the first time in his adult life, had a home to go to—the home of Elizabeth Schuyler, his intended bride.

Their wedding took place on December 14 in the large and magnificent mansion owned by Betsey's father, located on the banks of the Hudson River at Albany, New York. That day the house was crowded with well-wishers and members of Betsey's family. The only "family" representing Hamilton, however, was another Washington aide, Hamilton's good friend Colonel James McHenry.

When Hamilton had to leave a tearful bride behind after less than a month of marriage, he promised she could soon join him at headquarters, then established in New Windsor, New York.

He pointed out that by the time she arrived, other wives would be at headquarters, including "Lady" Washington. And that was indeed the case when Betsey reached New Windsor early in 1781.

Soon afterward, however, there was an unexpected change in Hamilton's situation. As he put it in a letter to Betsey's father, "I am no longer a member of the General's family."

Weary of his four-year stint at headquarters, Hamilton had tried for months to arrange for a transfer to another post of equal or higher rank. Washington, however, always seemed to have an acceptable reason to keep Hamilton on his staff. Eventually, Hamilton realized that some day he would break with Washington.

In his letter to Philip Schuyler, Hamilton explained that tempers had flared after he and the general passed each other on the stairs of a little stone house Washington occupied on the banks of the Hudson.

"He told me he wanted to speak to me," Hamilton wrote Schuyler. "I answered that I would wait upon him immediately. I went below, and delivered Mr. (Tench) Tilghman a letter to be sent to the commissary, containing an order of pressing and interesting nature."

On his way back to Washington, Hamilton was stopped briefly by Lafayette. When he reached Washington, the general said angrily, "Colonel Hamilton, you have kept me waiting at the head of the stairs these ten minutes. I must tell you, sir, you treat me with disrespect."

Hamilton said he replied, "I am not conscious of it, sir, but since you have thought it necessary to tell me so, we part."

According to Hamilton, Washington responded, "Very well, sir, if it be your choice."

Less than an hour later, Colonel Tilghman went to Hamilton with what amounted to an apology and the hope that the flareup could be forgotten. Hamilton had decided, however, that it was time to take a stand and told Tilghman he was leaving Washington's staff but would not do so until a replacement could be found.

Hamilton's father-in-law, however, urged Hamilton to remain at his post. "The French already know and acknowledge your abilities, and how necessary you are to the General," Schuyler added. "Indeed, how will the loss be replaced? He will, if you leave him, have not one gentleman sufficiently versed in French to convey his ideas.

"Make the sacrifice. The greater it is, the more glorious to you."

Hamilton didn't agree. And he did not change his mind.

For five days, Hamilton, who was fluent in French, dutifully acted as interpreter for Washington during conferences with the French high command aboard the eighty-gun flagship *Duc de Bourgogne* in the harbor at Newport.

When it was over, Hamilton obtained leave and went to his wife in Albany.

But he was not happy. He wanted to return to the army not as a member of Washington's staff but as commander of an artillery or infantry unit.

Toward the end of June, Hamilton learned that French troops stationed at Newport were marching southward to join the Americans camped at Dobbs Ferry, New York. Knowing that a major campaign was underway, Hamilton bade Betsey a cheery good-bye, told her not to worry, and rode downriver.

Arriving at the American camp close to dark on July 8, he was warmly greeted by General Benjamin Lincoln and quartered with his Massachusetts officers.

Hamilton soon learned that Cornwallis now had an army of 7,000 in Virginia—an army almost double the size of the American forces in the south.

It was also noted that Cornwallis was establishing a base on the Chesapeake at Yorktown, where he could easily be supplied and reinforced by ship.

The joint French-American plan, Hamilton was told, called for an attack against New York. This would prevent Clinton from giving Cornwallis any more support. In fact, it was hoped, Cornwallis might be forced to return troops to Clinton.

Either way, a strong move against Clinton would allow Lafayette, Wayne, and Greene to keep American hopes alive in the south until the main French fleet arrived, although no one knew when that might be.

Hamilton was cheered by these developments. By now, he was certain, Washington would have found a field command for him.

He was wrong. There was no place for him in the line, he was told the morning after his arrival in Lincoln's camp. Hamilton then became so angry he wrote Washington a harsh letter and resigned from the army.

But a day later, everything changed. "This morning," he wrote Betsey, "Colonel Tilghman came to me in the General's name and pressed me to retain my commission, with the assurance that he would endeavor, by all means, to give me a command . . ."

While he knew it wouldn't make Betsey happy, Hamilton said, he "consented."

At the end of July, nineteen months after he first requested combat duty, Hamilton took command of a battalion of light troops that was to be part of an advance corps.

∞

By early August, some 5,000 French troops had joined about 7,000 Americans and were preparing to attack New York as soon as the French fleet arrived from the West Indies.

On August 14, however, word came that the French fleet was not going to New York, but to the Chesapeake. The admiral, Comte Paul de Grasse, said he would arrive by September 3 and must leave the area by October 15.

It appeared to the Americans that they now had a golden opportunity to trap and conquer Cornwallis's army. To succeed, however, two things had to happen: 1) The French fleet must arrive in the Chesapeake ahead of the British navy to cut off a Cornwallis escape from Yorktown by sea, and 2) A land force must also prevent Cornwallis from escaping inland.

The allied armies soon began the harrowing 450-mile (724-km) land and water journey to Virginia. And with them went twenty-four-year-old Lieutenant Colonel Alexander Hamilton.

Having sailed down the Chesapeake in a flotilla of small boats, the allied armies from the north moved up the James River to land at Williamsburg, Virginia, on September 26, 1781. Two days later, Hamilton's brigade of light infantry, now assigned to Lafayette, led the way to the outskirts of Yorktown.

By then, De Grasse was in the Chesapeake, and Cornwallis, his back to the York River and the sea, was heavily fortified in the town behind high, thick walls. And stretching away in front of him was a vast, flat field that offered no cover. Here and there, however, were several British redoubts made of earthern walls that masked artillery and some fifty to one hundred soldiers. Encircling the redoubts were barriers of tree trunks and sharpened branches.

While several of the British redoubts were abandoned, two stubbornly remained manned. To allow the allies to mount a successful siege on the British fortifications, they would have to be eliminated.

The "honor" of leading one attack went to the French; the other to an officer selected from among the Americans.

Lafayette, as commander of the American right wing, selected Colonel Jean-Joseph Sourbader de Gimat, a Frenchman.

Hamilton was outraged. He appealed to Washington.

"I am senior to Gimat," he wrote the commander in chief. "And at the time planned for the attack, I'm officer of the day."

Washington ruled in Hamilton's favor.

∞

In the hours before the attack was launched on October 14, Hamilton told his men they would approach the redoubt from the right, while a second column under his old friend, John Laurens, would rush to the rear to cut off any attempt at an escape.

Guns, he instructed, were to be unloaded and bayonets fixed. There was to be no talking or unnecessary sound until the attack was discovered.

Shortly after midnight, six evenly spaced shots from allied guns sent Hamilton and his men on

76

As Cornwallis surrenders to Washington,
Hamilton stands by (third from right,
next to the white horse).

their way. As the two columns quickly closed in on the enemy redoubt, British watchdogs barked a warning, but by the time the enemy was fully alert, Hamilton's shouting, charging men were tearing away at the outer barriers and pouring over the parapet.

Overwhelmed, the British quickly surrendered. As a result, casualties were light on both sides. Meanwhile, the French had successfully taken the second redoubt.

The American and French soldiers now extended a trench to include both redoubts. By morning, the diggers had reached the river, giving allied gunners the ability to bombard the enemy lines from both frontal and side positions.

In a message to Congress, Washington said, "The works we have carried are of vast importance to us. From them we shall enfilade [rake with gunfire] the enemy's whole line."

And in his report of the American phase of the battle, Lafayette noted that Hamilton "commanded the whole advance corps" and that his "well-known talents and gallantry were on this occasion most conspicuous and serviceable."

Over the next two days, the allies moved scores of cannons into position and mounted a deadly and almost continuous bombardment of the British defenses.

On October 19, 1781, Cornwallis surrendered.

Part IV

After the victory at Yorktown, Hamilton obtained leave and rushed home to Albany, arriving there in time to celebrate his first wedding anniversary. A month later—on January 22, 1782—Betsey gave birth to a baby boy. He was named Philip.

When the baby was seven months old, Hamilton proudly wrote a friend that Philip was "a very fine gentleman, the most agreeable in his conversation and manners of any I ever knew.

"His features are good, his eye is not only sprightly and expressive, but full of benignity," Hamilton added. "His attitude by sitting is by connoisseurs esteemed graceful and he has a method of waving his little hand that announces the future orator. He stands, however, rather awkwardly and his legs have not the delicate slimness of his father's. It is feared he may never excel in dancing, which is probably the only accomplishment in which he will not be a model. If he has any fault in manners, he laughs too much."

Later, Hamilton wrote the same friend that he had become "entirely domestic. I lose all taste for the pursuits of ambition," he added. "I sigh for nothing but the company of my wife and baby. The ties of duty alone, or imagined duty, keep me from renouncing public life altogether. It is, however, probable that I may not be any longer actively engaged in it."

Luckily for America, however, Hamilton did remain "actively engaged" in public life.

Although a state of war still existed in America and elsewhere, peace commissioners representing England, France, Spain, and the United States began working in Paris to bring hostilities to an end.

During this tense and uneasy period, the British military forces in the United States seemed content to stay within their posts in and around New York City; Charleston, South Carolina; Savannah, Georgia; and various parts of the Northwest Territory.

And since the French army and navy had left for home after Yorktown, the Americans could do nothing but keep a watchful eye on the enemy.

By April 1782, when it became clear to Hamilton that he would not be called back to the army, which was now camped at Newburgh, New York, he plunged into an intensive study of law at the Albany offices of his old friend, Robert

Troup. In three months, the Supreme Court of New York said Hamilton, "having on examination been found of sufficient ability and competent learning," could practice law in New York State.

After a brief stint as the receiver of state taxes for the Continental treasury, Hamilton was elected by the state legislature to a seat in Congress. In a letter to John Laurens, Hamilton said, "Peace made, my dear friend, a new scene opens. The object then will be to make our independence a blessing. To do this, we must secure our union on solid foundations, a herculean task, and to effect it mountains of prejudice must be leveled!"

He urged Laurens, who was still in the army, to "quit your sword, my friend, put on the toga, come to Congress."

"We know each other's sentiments, our views are the same; we have fought side by side to make America free," he added. "Let us hand in hand struggle to make her happy."

But by the end of 1782, Hamilton's dream of establishing a "free" and "happy" America seemed headed for disaster. The reason was debt. The nation owed enormous sums of money to those who had supported eight years of war: farmers, merchants, businessmen, foreign countries, and the army.

There was only one way to reduce or eliminate these debts, and that was by taxation. Robert Morris, superintendent of finance, promptly recommended the imposition of poll taxes, land taxes, and a tax on imports.

Although Congress could only levy taxes with the unanimous consent of the states, Morris was sure "the sacred bonds of national faith and honor" would motivate the states to support his program.

He was wrong.

"It was like preaching to the dead," he said after his efforts failed.

The only tax that appeared to survive was the tax on imports. But while twelve states agreed to this single tax, Rhode Island, the smallest state, refused. And when Virginia, the largest state, decided to reverse its vote of approval, Hamilton came to an inescapable conclusion: The United States was bankrupt.

Late in 1782, the officers with the army at Newburgh, New York, sent a delegation to Congress in Philadelphia to present a petition that called for prompt payment of long-overdue pay and pensions.

The petition was politely worded, but firm in tone.

> To the United States assembled . . .
> "We, the officers of the Army of the United States, in behalf of ourselves and our brethren the soldiers, beg leave freely to state to the supreme power, our head and sovereign, the distress under which we labor. Our embarrassments thicken so fast that many of us are unable to go further.

Shadows have been offered to us, while the substance has been gleaned by others. The citizens murmur at the greatness of their taxes, and no part reaches the Army. We have borne all that men can bear. Our property is expended; our private resources are at an end. We therefore beg that a supply of money may be forwarded to the Army as soon as possible. . . .

Failure to do so may have fatal effects.

Congress responded by appointing a "Grand Committee" to look into the army's complaints. Members included Hamilton, Secretary of Finance Robert Morris, and a young congressman from Virginia named James Madison.

In mid-February, word came that a preliminary peace treaty had been reached between the United States and England. When it was signed, Congress would order the army to disband.

Would the army go home peacefully believing it would never receive its pay or pensions? Or would it use its weapons to obtain justice?

Alarmed by the possibility that the army might overthrow the government, Hamilton decided not to wait for the answer.

Although he had not communicated with him for months, Hamilton turned to the one man who might be able to control the army—George Washington.

In a lengthy, impassioned letter written to the commander in chief on February 7, Hamilton said the nation's financial condition "was perhaps never more critical" and that there was never a period in the Revolution that called for more "wisdom and decision in Congress."

He said Congress was not governed "by reason or foresight, but circumstances," the circumstances being that Congress had no power. Hamilton then appealed to Washington to use his influence to bring the situation under control and to "take direction" of efforts to satisfy the army's claims.

"It is of moment to public tranquillity, that your Excellency should preserve the confidence of the Army without losing that of the people," Hamilton argued. "This will enable you in case of extremity to guide the torrent, and to bring order, perhaps even good, out of confusion."

Washington was not convinced. In his reply, he said, "The predicament in which I stand as a citizen and soldier is as critical and delicate as can well be conceived. The sufferings of a complaining army on one hand and the inability of Congress and tardiness of the states on the other, are forebodings of evil."

Washington added, however, that he did not believe the officers would go beyond "the bounds of reason and moderation." As a result, he would not lead the army against the states.

On receiving Washington's response, Hamilton feared the worst. Soon, to his dismay, an explosive development emerged from the camp of an old enemy, a development that posed a serious threat to the life of the budding United States.

∞

An unsigned handbill distributed to the officers at Newburgh on March 10, 1783, carried a clear and ominous message—the officers might mutiny.

If the army wasn't paid and peace with England was achieved, the handbill warned, "Nothing can separate you (the army) from your arms but death."

If, on the other hand, the nation continued at war, the army was to "retire to some unsettled country" and leave the country defenseless, the unknown writer added.

Included in the handbill was an unauthorized call to all officers to attend a meeting the following day. These mutinous messages came from the camp of the army's second in command: General Horatio Gates, the "hero" of Saratoga and a leading member of the group that had tried to unseat Washington in 1777–1778.

The implication? If Washington wouldn't lead the army in its fight for back pay and pensions, Gates would.

Goaded into action, Washington canceled the unauthorized meeting, called one of his own, and, in an impassioned speech, convinced his officers that Congress would meet their demands. The threat of a mutiny that could have toppled the government passed quickly.

But the new nation's troubles were far from over.

Hamilton left Congress in August 1783. Three months later, he moved Betsey and his son from Albany to a new residence at 57 Wall Street in New York City, where he resumed the practice of law.

By then, the peace treaty was signed and the British had evacuated the city. And by then a new kind of "war" had erupted—a struggle for economic survival.

To Alexander Hamilton, the failure of Congress to properly feed, clothe, arm, and pay the Continental army (and others) during the Revolutionary War spelled disaster for the new nation. He was convinced that the Articles of Confederation, which at that time was the rule of the land, had to be changed.

Under the Articles, Congress was a single body that acted as a committee with a rotating chairman (president). Its members were appointed by the states. And in dealing with the thirteen increasingly independent and uncooperative states, Congress was virtually powerless.

Publicly and privately, Hamilton spoke out repeatedly about the need for a strong "national" government. In a newspaper article he signed as "The Continentalist," Hamilton wrote, "There is something noble and magnificent in the perspective of a great Federal Republic, closely linked to the pursuit of a common interest, tranquil and prosperous at home, respectable abroad."

This print shows Wall Street in 1783,
the year that Hamilton moved there with
his family to practice law.

But, he warned, there was also something "small and contemptible in the prospect of a number of petty states, with only the appearance of union, jarring, jealous and perverse, without any determined direction, fluctuating and unhappy at home, weak and insignificant by their dissenions in the eyes of other nations."

How could a nation continue to exist if it couldn't pay its debts? Hamilton asked over and over. And what would happen to the country if the newly independent states were not solidly united under a federal government?

Hamilton was convinced that unless the central government was somehow strengthened, the United States would dissolve and the Revolution would have been fought for nothing.

Hamilton wasn't alone in his concern for the survival of the United States. Among those who supported his views was his former commander in chief, George Washington, with whom friendly relations had been restored.

Washington told Hamilton in a letter, "No man in the United States can be more deeply impressed with the necessity of reform in our present Confederation than myself. No man perhaps has felt the bad effects of it more sensibly. More than half of the perplexities I have experienced in the course of my command, and almost the whole of the difficulties and distress of the Army, have their origin here."

But soon there was a ray of hope. In January 1786, Virginia invited her sister states to a convention "to consider how far a uniform system in their commercial regulations may be necessary to their common interest and permanent harmony."

A "uniform system" that would involve all the states? If adopted, that would mean a "national" system!

Four months later, the New York legislature named five commissioners to attend the convention, which was to be held in Annapolis, Maryland. Hamilton was one of them.

The Annapolis convention was to be held in Maryland's state house on September 4. But by then, three of the New York commissioners had decided not to attend, believing it would be a waste of time. Others arrived as much as a week late.

Hamilton and the only other New York delegate, Egbert Benson, left New York on horseback on September 2 and did not arrive in Annapolis until nine days later.

Being late didn't matter. Only twelve delegates, representing five of the thirteen states, attended the session, which didn't open until September 11, 1786.

With John Dickinson of Pennsylvania serving as chairman and Tench Coxe (also of Pennsylvania) in the role of secretary, the delegates quickly realized that with eight states absent it would be futile to offer any specific recommendations about interstate commercial regulations.

Instead, they tackled what they saw as the nation's fundamental problem: the Articles of Confederation. After considerable discussion, the convention appointed Hamilton as chair of a committee that would develop an "address" to Congress and the thirteen states.

This document, written by Hamilton with considerable help from James Madison of Virginia, called on the states to send delegates to a convention to be held in Philadelphia in 1787 to "devise such further provisions as shall appear to them necessary to render the Constitution of the Federal Government adequate to the exigencies of the Union."

But Hamilton was worried. If only five states sent delegates to Annapolis, how could anyone reasonably expect thirteen to be represented at a constitutional convention in Philadelphia the following year?

Only days after Hamilton's return to New York from Annapolis, the nation seemed to fall apart. There were riots in New England as farmers fought to keep their land from being confiscated by people they had borrowed from during the war.

In Massachusetts, for example, some four hundred men surrounded and threatened a court that was about to rule in favor of a bank foreclosure. During the melee, the leader of the mob was heard to yell, "I'm going to give the court four hours to agree to our terms. If they don't, we will force them to it." The court hastily adjourned.

And angry farmers, led by a war veteran named Daniel Shays, also marched to Springfield and attempted to seize the state arsenal. Only the timely arrival of the state militia thwarted their plans.

The root cause of all this unrest was a drastic drop in the value of paper money. To Hamilton, there was only one solution to the nation's rapidly increasing financial woes: a stronger union.

Hamilton knew from his experience during the war, however, that the loyalty of the average American was first to his home, then to his community, and finally to his state. To most, the idea that people should support a national government was quite new.

When he was elected to begin serving a term as an assemblyman in the New York legislature in January 1787, Hamilton immediately began pleading with his colleagues to take the steps necessary to establish a stronger federal government.

First, he said, Congress must have the authority to raise money through taxes.

> Can our national character be preserved without paying our debts? Can the union subsist without revenue? Have we realized the consequences which would attend its dissolution?
>
> If these states are not united under a Federal Government, they will infallibly have wars with each other; and their division will subject them to all the mischiefs of foreign influence and intrigue.

He said the western states were ripe for conquest by a foreign power, such as England or Spain, if the states failed to remain united. And then he warned: "Let us cast our eye upon the map of this state [New York], intersected from one extremity to the other by a large navigable river [the Hudson]. In the event of a rupture [among other states], what is to hinder our metropolis [New York City] from being prey to our neighbors?"

"Wars with each other," he added, "would beget standing armies—a source of more real danger to our liberties than all the powers that could be conferred upon the representatives of the Union. And wars with each other would lead to opposite alliances with foreign powers, and plunge us into the labyrinths of European politics."

To Hamilton's anger and dismay, the legislature ignored him.

Hamilton was very active while serving in the New York State legislature. He successfully sponsored a bill establishing the University of New York, tried but failed to get Vermont (then a part of New York) admitted as another state, and tackled the sensitive issue of divorce.

At the time, only a legislative act could dissolve a marriage in New York State. Hamilton introduced and won passage of a bill that would permit divorce on the grounds of adultery; this law would remain in effect for more than a hundred and fifty years.

When Congress called for a constitutional convention in May 1787, Hamilton was concerned that New York might not participate. Governor Clinton, after all, had said after the Annapolis convention that "the Confederation as it stands is equal to the purposes of the Union."

In response to Hamilton's pleas, New York reluctantly decided to send Hamilton, Robert Yates, and John Lansing Jr. to the Convention as its delegates. But there was a catch. Each state would have only one vote, and Yates and Lansing were Clinton supporters.

"They mean to nullify my vote," Hamilton said.

He was right.

∞

Hamilton left New York for Philadelphia in mid-May accompanied by Robert Yates, one of his two fellow delegates. John Lansing was to follow a few days later.

Slowed by spring rains, muddy roads, and dangerous water crossings, the pair didn't reach Philadelphia until May 18, four days after the scheduled opening of the convention.

After seeing to the care of their horses and going to rooms reserved at a tavern called the Indian Queen, the two walked to the State House only to find that the convention lacked a quorum, or majority, and had failed to open.

Yates commented with a smirk that it looked like "another Annapolis."

Seven days after Hamilton's arrival, however, a quorum was reached and the delegates promptly

This is how Philadelphia looked when Hamilton arrived there for the Constitutional Convention in 1787.

elected George Washington as president of the convention; selected a secretary, a doorkeeper, a messenger; and named the rules committee.

Two days later, behind closed doors and sealed windows, the convention began a secret debate that would ultimately change the face and history of not only America, but the world.

∞

While fifty-five delegates had been named to attend the convention, only twenty-nine were on hand at the opening session. Still, enough states were represented to allow the convention to proceed on schedule.

With an average age of forty-four, these delegates were younger than those who had adopted the Declaration of Independence eleven years before. Like the earlier group, however, this one was well-educated and knowledgeable about government. And while the delegates were generally of a practical mind, they had strong opinions, especially about states' rights versus the rights of a national government.

The first order of business addressed on May 28, 1787, was the set of rules drafted by a committee headed by sixty-year-old George Wythe of Virginia, one of the signers of the Declaration of Independence.

After digesting the rules, the delegates adjourned. The next day, Tuesday, May 29, the fireworks began.

∞

The first speaker on that historic day was handsome thirty-two-year-old Edmund Randolph, governor of Virginia and head of that state's seven-man delegation.

"To prevent the fulfillment of the prophecies of the downfall of the United States, it is our duty to inquire into the defects of the [Articles] of Confederation and the requisite properties of the Government now to be framed; the danger of the situation and its remedy," Randolph began.

After a slight pause, during which the delegates shifted in their seats, he went on, "The Confederation was made in the infancy of the science of constitutions, when the inefficiency of requisitions was unknown; when no commercial discord had arisen among the states; when no rebellion like that in Massachusetts had broken out; when foreign debts were not urgent; when the havoc of paper money had not been foreseen; when treaties had not been violated; and when nothing better could have been conceded by states jealous of their sovereignty."

Randolph then pointed out the defects in the Articles of Confederation, saying it could not prevent or conduct a war, nor prevent a quarrel between states, suppress a rebellion, collect taxes, or enable the nation to compete commercially with other nations.

He also noted that the Articles of Confederation could not "be claimed to be paramount to the state constitutions; so there is the prospect of anarchy from the inherent laxity of government."

He said the only cure for all of these weaknesses in the Articles was a government based on "the republican principle."

Startled, the delegates looked at each other with frowns and raised eyebrows. Did Randolph mean they should ignore their mission, which was to revise the Articles of Confederation? Or was he saying the Articles should be scrapped in favor of a new government? If so, what kind of government?

The answers came in a presentation that took Randolph almost four hours to deliver. For the most part, delegate Hamilton was pleased. But he had serious misgivings, as did others.

The "Virginia Resolves" introduced to the convention by Randolph were mainly the work of James Madison. They were hammered out in various Philadelphia taverns by the Virginia delegates during the eleven days the convention was stalled for lack of a quorum.

When the fifteen resolves were presented, attention became focused on three proposals:

1. "A national legislature" that would "consist of two branches, of which the members of the first or democratic house ought to be elected by the people of the several states; of the second, by those of the first, out of persons nominated by the individual [state] legislatures."

2. "A national executive [President], chosen by the national legislature and ineligible for a second term."

3. "A national judiciary [court system] to consist of supreme and inferior tribunals; to be chosen by the national legislature."

As presented, these three resolves established a framework for the proposed government. This framework immediately sparked a heated controversy among the delegates.

If the "people of the several states" were to elect members to the "first house" (the House of Representatives), that clearly implied that the states with the highest population would dominate the smaller states.

This resolve also destroyed a key principle of the Articles of Confederation, which held that each state should have an equal vote, regardless of size.

But as the proposals were digested and debated, one thing became clear: Most, but definitely not all, of the delegates favored getting rid of the Articles of Confederation and creating a new form of government. Most also seemed to realize that trying to revise the Articles, as they had been instructed to do, was hopeless.

As James Wilson of Pennsylvania said, "To give additional weight to an old building is to hasten its ruin."

And most—again, not all—favored a startling and unprecedented idea imbedded in the proposals: the idea that government should be put in the hands of the governed.

∽

Hamilton saw many defects in the Virginia Resolves, but in the early days of the convention he had little to say, and for a very good reason: Governor Clinton's hand-picked delegates, Yates and Lansing, constantly canceled out his vote.

Despite his helpless position, Hamilton was determined to speak, but not until all the proposals appeared to be out in the open.

That opportunity came after William Paterson of New Jersey rose to offer a different scheme of government, warning that, "New Jersey will never confederate on the plan before the committee [the Virginia plan]. She would be swallowed up. I would rather submit to a monarch, to a despot, than to such a fate. I will not only oppose the plan here, but on my return home do everything in my power to defeat it there."

Under Paterson's plan, designed to favor the small states, Congress would be a single body, its members elected by the states they represented.

Although New York was one of the larger states, Yates and Lansing favored Paterson's plan.

Lansing also insisted that the delegates did not have the authority to destroy the Articles of Confederation. "You can only change them," he insisted. "If New York suspected an attempt would be made to form a national government, it would not have sent its delegates to Philadelphia."

After three days of debate, the New Jersey plan was defeated. Now it was Hamilton's turn.

At Washington's opening gavel on June 18, Hamilton rose and spoke for six hours. During this discourse, he found fault with both the Virginia plan and the Paterson plan.

Some of Hamilton's remarks were included in notes taken by several delegates:

"I have grave doubts whether a national government on the Virginia Plan can be effectual."

"The Virginia Plan is but pork still, with a little change of sauce."

"The voice of the people has been said to be the voice of God, but it is not true in fact. The people are turbulent and ever-changing; they seldom judge or determine right."

"The general government must not only have a strong soul, but strong organs by which that soul is to operate. The best form of government, not attainable by us, but the model to which we should approach as near as possible, is the British Constitution."

"Men love power. Give power to the many, they will oppress the few. Give all power to the few, they will oppress the many."

During his speech, Hamilton listed the items in his plan:

- Election of a president for life with the power of veto over all legislation.

- Election of senators by "electors" for life. (Electors are those given the sole right to vote for a candidate for public office. Today, they are members of what is known as the electoral college. Electoral votes decide the presidency and vice presidency.)

- Appointment of state governors by the president; governors to hold office for life.

- Members of the lower house to be elected by the people for a term of three years.

Hamilton said his plan "constitutes an elective monarch; but by making the executive subject to impeachment, the term 'monarch' cannot apply."

While Hamilton's plan was greeted by silence and no action was taken, many were impressed. Gouverneur Morris of Pennsylvania, for example, said the speech was "the most able and impressive" he had ever heard. Another delegate, William Samuel Johnson, also thought well of Hamilton's "boldness and decision" but found that he had been "praised by everybody but supported by none."

Since he had finally had his say and found that Yates and Lansing had rendered him powerless, Hamilton went home. The rest of the New York delegation soon followed.

But Hamilton's speech had an important effect on the convention: The delegates now seemed convinced that a completely new national constitution was needed and instead of discussing only its form, they began to concentrate on its strength and durability.

On reaching New York, Hamilton wrote to Washington, saying that the many conversations he had with people during his ride home convinced him "there has been an astonishing revolution for the better in the minds of the people."

"The prevailing apprehension among thinking men is that the Convention, far from a fear of shocking the popular opinion, may not go far enough," he added. "Men in (public) office are indeed taking all possible pains to give an unfavorable impression of the Convention, but the current is running strongly the other way."

Such was not the case at the convention, however, Washington replied on July 10. "I almost despair of seeing a favourable issue to the proceedings of the Convention, and do therefore repent having had any agency in the business.

"The men who oppose a strong & energetic government are, in my opinion, narrow-minded politicians, or are under the influence of local views . . "

"I am sorry you went away," he added. "I wish you were back. The crisis is equally important and alarming, and no opposition under such circumstances should discourage exertions till the signature is fixed."

Part of the crisis Washington referred to stemmed from disagreement on the appropriate representation in the two houses of Congress. After an intensive battle, Hamilton learned later, the convention accepted a compromise suggested by Benjamin Franklin: In the upper house (Senate) the states would have equal representation, while all money bills would originate in the lower house (House of Representatives).

But when the convention turned its attention to representation in the lower house, it encountered an explosive issue—slavery.

∽

While some argued that selection of members to the lower house should be on the basis of individual wealth, the majority felt it should be based on population. Clearly, this meant the more populous states would dominate the small.

Unless slaves were counted, as had already been proposed, Pennsylvania, New York, Massachusetts, and Virginia would also wield more power in Congress than the sparsely settled slave-holding states in the south, such as South Carolina and Georgia.

Linked to this argument was another critical question: Should the new government allow the importation of slaves to continue? If it did, and slaves were counted, the slave-holding states would continue to gain power.

During the debate, it became clear that unless there was a compromise on issues concerning slavery, the southern states would join the small states of the north and the effort to write a constitution would collapse.

As Pierce Butler of South Carolina put it, "The security the southern states want is that their Negroes may not be taken from them."

On July 12, the majority finally agreed that representation to the lower house should be based on the number of free persons and three-fifths of "all other persons" (slaves) in each state.

Scores of other issues had yet to be ironed out, however. To speed the work, a Committee of Detail was chosen to try to draft a constitution during a ten-day recess.

Early in August, the committee made its report. Slavery again became an issue when Luther Martin of Maryland insisted that the slave trade (the business of importing slaves) should be prohibited or subject to import taxes.

Martin felt that if the importation of slaves was unrestricted "it weakens one part of the union which other parts are bound to protect."

Slavery, he said, "is inconsistent with the principles of the Revolution and dishonorable to the American character."

This was too much for John Rutledge of South Carolina. "Religion and humanity have nothing to do with this question!" Rutledge barked. "Interest alone is the governing principle with nations. The true question at present is whether the southern states shall, or shall not, be a party to the Union."

It was pointed out, however, that the northern states would object to paying an import tax on various goods if the south were allowed to import slaves without a tax. Soon, the delegates compromised as they had on the issue of representation: The northern states would pay the import tax, but the slave trade would be abolished after twenty years.

Because he now felt strongly that New York should have a vote in shaping the constitution, Hamilton asked Yates and Lansing to return with him to the convention. They refused. Hamilton went back to Philadelphia anyway.

∞

Although New York had lost its vote with the absence of Yates and Lansing, Hamilton was given the opportunity to speak on several occasions as the convention rolled on, a clear indication that the delegates had great respect for his intelligence and ability.

At one point, Hamilton argued for a larger representation in the House of Representatives. "The fabric of the American empire ought to rest on the solid basis of the 'consent of the people,'" he said. "The streams of national power ought to flow immediately from that pure original fountain of all legislative authority."

On another occasion, Hamilton said "liberty" meant that men should have a right to share in the government. "Being naturally equal, every man having evidence of attachment to, and permanent common interest with society, ought to share in all its rights and privileges."

By early September, after almost four months of debate, agreement had been reached on every major issue but one: the executive.

How should the executive be elected? How old should he be to be eligible? Should he be native born? What should be the length of his term? Should there be one, two, or three members of the executive office?

After long, heated arguments about many such questions, agreement was reached on September 7 and included these principle points: The president would be chosen by electors from each state, the term of office would be four years, and the number of terms unlimited.

Five days later, the Constitution was completed, printed, and ready for signature. Now, if the states ratified the document, the nation would have a new form of government. But there was an unexpected hitch; Virginia's Edmund Randolph moved for a second convention!

"The states should have the right to amend the Constitution in its present form," Randolph declared. Then he added that the amendments, whatever they turned out to be, together with the Constitution, should be submitted to another general convention for a final decision.

"If not," he said, "I cannot sign the Constitution."

George Mason, also of Virginia, and Elbridge Gerry of Connecticut, agreed with Randolph. After Randolph's motion was seconded, however, the states voted an emphatic "Nay!"

So on September 17, 1787, thirty-eight delegates representing eleven states (Rhode Island did not send delegates to the convention) put their signatures beneath the text of this remarkable and unprecedented document. True to their word, delegates Randolph, Gerry, and Mason did not sign, but that did not affect the votes of the states they represented.

With New York officially absent, however, Alexander Hamilton signed as a private individual. In doing so, he made three things clear:

- He was acting against the wishes of the most popular and powerful man in New York State, Governor George Clinton.

- He was ready to defend and support the Constitution.

- He hoped to play a role in the new government—if and when it was born.

Even before Congress sent copies of the Constitution to the states for ratification, it had begun to divide the public into two groups. Those who supported the document were called "Federalists," and those who opposed it, "anti-Federalists."

Obviously, the anti-Federalists did not like a strong central government and wanted only to revise the Articles of Confederation.

The heaviest blows came from Governor Clinton and his followers and several prominent Virginians, including Richard Henry Lee and Patrick Henry.

Realizing the Constitution would spark a battle for public opinion, Hamilton teamed up with John Jay of New York (the former secretary of foreign affairs) and James Madison to write a series of "Federalist Papers" explaining the merits of the proposed government.

The first of the articles appeared in the *New York Independent Journal* on October 27, 1787. Written by Hamilton, it began:

> After an unequivocal experience of the inefficiency of the subsisting [current] federal government, you are called upon to deliberate on a new Constitution for the United States of America. The subject speaks its own importance; comprehending in its consequences, nothing less than the existence of

the Union, the safety and welfare of the parts of which it is composed, the fate of an empire in many respects the most interesting in the world. It has been frequently remarked that it seems to have been reserved to the people of this country, by their conduct and example, to decide the important questions; whether societies of men are really capable or not, of establishing good government from reflection and choice, or whether they are forever destined to depend for their political constitutions on accident and force.

"My countrymen," he added, "I own to you after having given it an attentive consideration, I am clearly of the opinion it is in your interest to adopt [the Constitution]. I am convinced that this is the safest course for your liberty, your dignity, and your happiness."

The essay was signed "Publius" after Publius Valerius, a hero of ancient Rome who established a republican government after the fall of Rome's last king. Eighty-four "Publius" essays would follow, most of them written by Hamilton.

Shortly after the first article appeared, Delaware became the first state to ratify the Constitution. And before the end of 1787, Pennsylvania and New Jersey followed. The ninth state, New Hampshire, voted in favor of the Constitution on June 17, 1788.

Technically, with the approval of nine states, the Constitution was now ratified. Realistically, however, there would not be a new government unless two of the remaining four—Virginia and New York—also ratified, since they were, by far, the two largest states. And without them, most agreed, the Union could not survive.

∞

"'We the people?' Who authorizes gentlemen to speak the language of 'we the people' instead of 'we the states'? The people gave the Convention no power to use their name!"

So cried fifty-two-year-old Patrick Henry as the Virginia ratification convention opened with a reading of the Constitution in June 1788.

Henry's remarks triggered a debate that lasted for three weeks. This often-heated debate found James Madison calmly answering questions and giving the rationale for many of the decisions made at the Constitutional Convention.

Surprisingly, Edmund Randolph, who had refused to sign the Constitution unless a second convention was held, changed his position. A second convention, he said, might bring "inevitable ruin to the Union." He also favored the Constitution if it included a Bill of Rights.

After Madison promised his support for such an amendment, Virginia ratified 89 to 79.

Still, it was clear that even if Rhode Island and North Carolina joined the other ten, New York must ratify if there was to be a new United States. That meant Federalist hopes rested on the shoulders of one man: Alexander Hamilton.

Many believed that if wealthy and heavily populated New York State were to reject the Constitution and remain independent, the Union envisioned at the Constitutional Convention would not work.

New York was the nation's busiest trade center with a large harbor and abundant waterways. It was also strategically located between New England and the southern states and could easily form an alliance with a foreign power.

But Governor Clinton and his followers seemed unconcerned. At the upcoming state ratification convention only nineteen of the sixty-five delegates were Federalists.

On June 16, when the results in Virginia and New Hampshire were still unknown, two sloops left New York City for Poughkeepsie, where the state convention was to be held.

Hamilton, aboard the sloop bearing the Federalist supporters, looked across to the second sloop, which was carrying their opponents, and remarked, "The more I can penetrate the views of the anti-federalist party in this state, the more I dread the consequence of the non-adoption of the Constitution by any of the other states; and the more I fear eventual disunion and civil war."

Since Hamilton was the lone delegate from New York to sign the Constitution, he took the lead in reviewing it at the state convention when it opened on June 17.

As Hamilton proceeded clause by clause, there were so many questions, speeches, and interruptions, the proceeding dragged on for three weeks.

At various times during the debate, Hamilton made these points:

"The establishment of a republican government is [above] all others the nearest and dearest to my own heart. The true principle of a republic is that people should choose whom they please to govern them."

"The great source of free government, popular election, should be perfectly pure, and [with] the most unbounded liberty allowed."

At one point, a Clinton spokesman complained that Federalism smacked of rule by an "aristocracy," adding that the "common man" would be left out of the proposed government.

"For my part," Hamilton responded, "I hardly know the meaning of the word [aristocracy] as it is applied. Who are the aristocracy among us? Where do we find men elevated to a perpetual rank above their fellow citizens, and possessing powers entirely independent of them? The arguments of the gentleman only go to prove that there are men who are rich, men who are poor, some who are wise, and others who are not—that indeed, every distinguished man is an aristocrat."

When it was argued that under the Constitution the central government would destroy state government, Hamilton responded: "Gentlemen indulge too many unreasonable apprehensions of dangers to the state governments. The state governments are essential to the form and spirit of the general system."

Returning to this theme later, Hamilton said, "The state governments possess inherent advantages, which will ever give them an influence and ascendancy over national government; and will forever preclude the possibility of federal encroachments. That their liberties can indeed be subverted to the federal head, is repugnant to every rule of political calculation."

Over and over again, Hamilton pointed out that the proposed government included "checks and balances." "One branch is balanced against the other and the whole is checked by the states," he said.

While mostly calm and gracious, Hamilton grew angry when one anti-Federalist called him "an ambitious man, a man unattached to the interests and insensible to the feelings of the people."

"I challenge those among you to point out an instance in which I have ever deviated from the line of public or private duty!" he cried. There was no answer.

The anti-Federalists, however, seemed unmoved by Hamilton's rhetoric.

Toward the end of June, when word spread that New Hampshire and Virginia had voted to adopt the Constitution, the Federalists in New York City began building floats and designing banners in preparation for a gigantic victory parade.

Surely New York would ratify, the Federalists thought. But the debate in Poughkeepsie went on and on. After several postponements, however, the parade got underway on July 23, 1788.

The centerpiece was a 27-foot (8-meter) replica of a seagoing frigate that bore the name *Hamilton*. Built by shipyard workers and carpenters, the ship, mounted on a carriage and manned by thirty seamen and marines, was pulled through the streets by ten horses.

The parade to celebrate New York State's ratification of the Constitution included a model of a ship named after the state's hero of the convention, Alexander Hamilton.

As one newspaper reported, the *Hamilton* began its voyage at ten in the morning after a thirteen-gun salute and "made a fine appearance, sailing with flowing sheets and full sails, down Broadway, the canvas waves dashing against her sides."

Among the thousands who watched, applauded, and cheered wildly as the ship rolled along firing its cannons was Nicholas Cruger, the St. Croix businessman who had been instrumental in launching Hamilton's career.

The parade, however, seemed premature; the anti-Federalists at the state convention in Poughkeepsie were by then insisting that a new federal convention be held to consider amendments.

After consulting with Madison, Hamilton said no to another convention. "Let another convention be called tomorrow," he argued, "let them meet twenty times—nay, twenty thousand times! They will have the same difficulties to encounter, the same clashing interests to reconcile." A second convention, he added, would "tear the Constitution to shreds," making it worthless.

By now, some anti-Federalists began to have doubts. Could New York really survive alone? And what if New York City and the lower counties withdrew from the state, ratified the Constitution, and joined the Union?

The end to the debate came on July 26, when New York ratified 30 to 27.

With that vote a new government for the United States was finally assured. For the first time in history, government would be placed in the hands of the governed.

Part V

When Hamilton returned to his growing family and law practice after the six-week campaign to get New York to ratify the Constitution, his thoughts dwelt on one subject: the new government of the United States and how it was to be shaped, and how it would function.

The most important feature, he felt, was the office of president. He knew, of course, that during the debates about the Constitution, most Americans had only one man in mind as president—George Washington, the hero of the Revolution. And he realized that many embraced the Constitution primarily because they were convinced that their untried form of government would be safe in Washington's hands.

Washington, however, was reluctant to leave his beloved Virginia home, Mount Vernon, and take on such enormous responsibility. Aware of the general's feelings, Hamilton wrote Washington in September 1788:

> Every public and personal consideration will demand from you an acquiescence in what will certainly be the unanimous wish of your country. Your acceptance will make an infinite difference in the respectability with which the government will begin its operations.

A few weeks later, Washington made a cautious reply that began, "If I should be persuaded to accept . . ."

This "iffy" answer convinced Hamilton that Washington had only to be pushed a little harder. "I feel a conviction that you will finally see your acceptance to be indispensable," he said bluntly in another letter. "I am not sure that your refusal would not throw everything into confusion. I am sure that it would have the worst effect imaginable." Under the circumstances, Hamilton said, Washington had "no option."

Persuaded by Hamilton, Madison, and others, Washington reluctantly allowed his name to go forward as a candidate.

Like all Federalists, Hamilton hoped to unite the country behind the new government. Since Washington was from the south, it seemed important to select a candidate from the north as vice president.

John Adams, long a power in the politics of Massachusetts and a strong Federalist, seemed the ideal choice. But Hamilton hesitated. He didn't like Adams. Adams, in Hamilton's view, did not give Washington his full support during the war and was jealous of the general. Finally, however, Hamilton said in a letter to James Madison that he had "concluded to support Mr. Adams."

When the ballots of the official electors were opened in New York's Federal Hall on April 6, 1789, before members of the newly organized House of Representatives and Senate, Washington, with sixty-nine votes, was certified as having been unanimously elected president; John Adams with thirty, as vice president.

Slowly and deliberately, the government began to take shape. Several bills became law. Amendments to the Constitution were put in motion. And the executive departments—war, foreign affairs, and treasury—were created, followed by the judiciary.

Then came the president's appointments to these posts: Henry Knox as secretary of war, Thomas Jefferson as secretary of foreign affairs, John Jay as Chief Justice of the Supreme Court, and Edmund Randolph as attorney general.

As history would prove, however, Washington's most important choice was the man who would be the nation's first secretary of the treasury, thirty-two-year-old Alexander Hamilton.

Of all the problems facing the infant United States in 1789, two were the most complicated, the least understood, and the most dangerous: worthless paper money and a mountain of debt.

To survive, let alone prosper, the nation's frail and declining financial health had to be secured. But how?

To find the answer, the House of Representatives turned to the secretary of the treasury only ten days after he took office. Since "an adequate provision of public credit" was deemed "of high importance to the national honor and prosperity," Hamilton's charge was to "prepare a plan for that purpose."

Under the act that established the treasury, Hamilton had to respond to such requests from either the House or Senate "in person or in writing." For his initial assignment, this was a daunting task because Hamilton first had to determine who the creditors were and how much was owed.

He then had to develop a plan to pay the creditors and, at the same time, find a sufficient source of income to keep the country afloat financially.

After three months of intensive study, Hamilton gave the House a daring, 40,000-word document titled "Report Relative to a Provision for the Support of Public Credit."

Hamilton concluded that the total foreign debt amounted to $11.7 million; the domestic debt $40.4 million; and the debt of the states, approximately $25 million. Thus, the total debt, including interest, came to about $77 million, a staggering sum at the time.

To pay this enormous debt, Hamilton proposed offering the nation's creditors new bonds at face value at varying rates of interest. He also proposed funding the debt with new foreign loans and establishing a wide range of federal taxes. In his report, Hamilton pointed out that "loans in times of public danger, especially from foreign wars," were an indispensable source of money "even to the wealthiest (of nations)."

And, he said, since it was necessary to borrow in emergencies on good terms, "the credit of a nation should be well established." To maintain good credit, however, a country had to give evidence of "good faith by a punctual performance of contracts," meaning it must pay debts when due.

"States, like individuals" who pay their debts "are respected and trusted," while those who don't are not, Hamilton said.

While most of his proposal was accepted, two elements caused a storm of controversy: "assumption" of all state debts by the federal government, and Hamilton's plan to pay in full the holders of a variety of certificates of credit issued during the war to farmers, soldiers, small businessmen, and others.

A month after Hamilton handed his report to Congress, it came under attack by the one man he thought was his (and Washington's) most important political ally: James Madison.

James "Jemmy" Madison was a short man, so short he couldn't be seen when other men of average height gathered around him. And when he spoke in Congress, his voice was so weak his listeners had a hard time hearing him. But listen they did. For Madison was a brilliant and thoughtful man.

On a gloomy day in February 1790, the thirty-nine-year-old Madison had the full attention of the House of Representatives when he rose from his seat.

First, Madison blasted Hamilton's plan to pay the full value of certificates to those who held them. Most of the certificates, he said, were issued to soldiers in lieu of pay, to farmers for food for the army, and to small merchants for supplies. As the war wore on and the nation suffered an economic depression, thousands of those who held certificates were forced to sell them to speculators at below their face value.

*James Madison, in a portrait painted
in the late 1820s*

That meant, Madison said, that the speculators would get rich at the expense of the original owners of the certificates. Madison then proposed a plan that would have the government pay some of the value of the certificates to the original holders—such as orphans, widows, and farmers—and the rest to the current holders.

Hamilton's backers scoffed at this plan of "discrimination." It was pointed out that the Dutch government had invested heavily in these certificates and that it would be next to impossible to identify the original holders. It was also noted that if Madison's plan was adopted, it could double the nation's debt. The proposal was easily defeated.

But Madison wasn't finished. He now attacked the proposal that the federal government should assume all the debts of the states. This was unfair, he said, because many states, his home state of Virginia included, had already paid their wartime debts. Why should states like Virginia be asked to pay (indirectly) the debts of other states, especially when those debts were in the hands of speculators?

In the midst of a roaring debate, Madison suddenly made this motion: If the federal government was going to pay the debts of delinquent states, it should also reimburse the states that had already paid their war debts!

This "paid and unpaid" issue deadlocked Congress for weeks. When it did, Hamilton's valiant efforts to get the nation's finances in order came to an abrupt halt.

Inevitably, the funding debate reached many areas of the country and began to shape public opinion. Madison's supporters, for example, now saw him as "the champion of the common man." One even urged a prominent painter named John Trumbull to produce a canvas that would show Madison "pleading the cause of Justice and Humanity in Congress, an angel whispering in his ear, and a group of widows, orphans and decrepit soldiers, contemplating him in ineffable delight."

Hamilton, on the other hand, was viewed as being the favorite of the wealthy, a man who "enabled the proud speculator to roll along in his gilded chariot while the hardy veteran who had fought and bled for your liberties was left to toil for his support, or to beg his bread from door to door."

For five months, the funding program remained stalled in Congress. But in June 1790, a chance encounter between a frustrated Hamilton and a new arrival to New York offered a ray of hope. The newcomer was Thomas Jefferson.

Thomas Jefferson and Alexander Hamilton did not have much in common. While Hamilton was small of stature, youthful, usually in high spirits, and carefully dressed in the latest fashion, Jefferson was tall, loose-jointed, reserved in manner, and seemed to wear clothes a size too small.

There were other differences, too. Hamilton was an excellent speaker and a brilliant debater. Jefferson was neither. Hamilton, born on foreign soil, was the illegitimate son of a shiftless Scot and a mother of questionable character. Although Jefferson's father was a farmer, his mother was a member of a wealthy and prominent Virginia family.

But Jefferson and Hamilton had one thing in common: Both had visions of the United States becoming a great nation. They were poles apart, however, as to how this was to be accomplished.

During the war, Jefferson was governor of Virginia. Later, he replaced Benjamin Franklin as minister to France. After returning home to take up his duties as secretary of foreign affairs in June 1790, Jefferson accidentally met Hamilton in front of Washington's residence in New York. He was shocked by what he saw.

"He was sober, haggard and dejected beyond all description, even his dress uncouth and neglected," the forty-seven-year-old Jefferson wrote later. He soon learned why.

When they met, Hamilton quickly told Jefferson the nation faced a serious crisis. His funding proposal, he said, had been defeated five times and if it went down again, the New England states and South Carolina might leave the Union. And whether or not this happened, another defeat meant he would resign.

Jefferson was shocked. Having just arrived from France he was only vaguely aware of the

This engraving of Thomas Jefferson was made in 1801, while he was president.

problems with the funding bill. And he did know that the House and Senate were deadlocked on where to locate a permanent capital.

Surely, Jefferson said, something could be done. Only if Madison were willing to change his position, which didn't appear likely, Hamilton responded glumly.

A few days later, Jefferson spoke to Hamilton again. Perhaps, he said, something could be worked out if they were to sit down to dinner with Madison. Hamilton agreed.

At the dinner meeting, a solution to Hamilton's funding dilemma soon emerged. Jefferson and Madison, it was revealed, wanted the permanent national capital to be located somewhere in the south. If Hamilton would support that idea, they would help pass the funding bill. Hamilton was hesitant; he said there would be problems because other states wanted the capital, principally New York and Pennsylvania.

By the time the trio parted, however, an agreement had been reached. Hamilton would use his influence to move the capital from New York to Philadelphia for ten years, then to a permanent site on the Potomac River in an undeveloped area shared by Virginia and Maryland. In turn, the two Virginians would support Hamilton's financial plan.

Since only a few votes were needed to pass both pieces of legislation, the compromise worked with this result: The Union was preserved, its economy was saved, and a permanent "federal District" of 10 square miles (26 square kilometers) was established.

By the time Hamilton and Betsey journeyed from New York to the temporary national capital at Philadelphia in the fall of 1790, they were the parents of four young children: Philip, 8; Angelica, 6; Alexander, 4; and James Alexander, 2.

Although the Hamiltons were living on the secretary's meager salary of $3,000 dollars a year, Betsey managed to stage a number of lively and well-attended parties for local residents and members of the new government.

Hamilton, according to one observer, "was frequently seen at the theater, assembly hall, and the card table, relaxing from the cares of state. No American statesman ever combined more gracefully the hard-working administrator with the social butterfly."

Hamilton certainly was hardworking. On December 14, only a week after Congress convened, Hamilton submitted another voluminous report to the nation's legislators. Like the report on public credit, it raised a storm of controversy that would have a profound effect on the nation.

In his second major proposal, Hamilton called on Congress to charter a national bank to be called the Bank of the United States. It was to be capitalized at (established at a value of) $10 million.

To the average American, this was a staggering sum of money since the three state banks then in existence had a total capitalization of less than $2 million.

Under Hamilton's proposal, the government was to put up $2 million of the bank's capital, while the rest would come from private investors. Essentially, the bank would be a safe place for the government to place its cash. It would also serve as a source of loans to cover operating expenses in periods between the receipt of tax revenue.

There was another critical condition: While five of the bank's twenty-five directors would represent the government, the bank would be managed by private citizens.

"To attach full confidence to an institution of this nature, it appears to be an essential ingredient in its structure, that it shall be under private, not public direction—under the guidance of individual interest, not of public policy," Hamilton said.

Hamilton was convinced that his proposal would put sound money in circulation, make more capital available, ease credit, and improve business conditions. In short, he believed the bank would serve national interests, as contrasted to state, local, or sectional interests.

When the proposal was put to a vote in the House of Representatives, it passed 39 to 20. It also passed in the Senate by about the same margin. In both houses, however, the majority of the "aye" votes were cast by representatives of the northern states, the "no" votes by those from the south.

Clearly, the bank bill was seen by many as favorable to the moneyed interests of the North and unfavorable to the agricultural interests of the south. (Logically or not, farmers saw bankers as their enemies, since they constantly had to borrow money from banks when crops were poor.)

Although the bank bill passed and went to President Washington for his signature, its opponents raised a disturbing and insistent cry that the bank bill was unconstitutional. Was it?

Before signing the measure, Washington turned to his cabinet and to James Madison, his most influential supporter in the House for the answer.

∞

James Madison agreed that the bank bill was unconstitutional. So did Thomas Jefferson, secretary of foreign affairs, and Edmund Randolph, the attorney general.

Before taking any action, however, the president asked Hamilton to comment on these objections so that Washington "could be fully possessed of the argument for and against the measure before I express an opinion of my own." While waiting for Hamilton's reply, Washington also asked Madison to prepare a veto message for him should he refuse to sign the bank bill.

Madison promptly wrote the following for the President's use: "I object to the bill because it is an essential principle of Government that powers not delegated [spelled out] by the Constitution cannot rightfully be exercised; because the power proposed by the bill to be exercised is not delegated; and because I cannot satisfy myself that it results from an expressed power by fair and safe rules of implication."

In the proposed message for the president, Madison was saying, in effect, that the Constitution did not contain any language anywhere that specifically gave the government the right and power to establish a bank.

Randolph, Jefferson, and other opponents of the bill put forth essentially the same argument, but added that only states could charter banks.

Almost overnight, Hamilton responded with a 15,000-word essay that declared in part: ". . . every power vested in a government is in its nature, sovereign, and includes, by force of the term, a right to employ all the means and requisite fairly applicable to the attainment of the ends of such power."

The Constitution, in other words, contained implied powers, Hamilton said. And in concluding his treatise, he pointed out that a national bank "has a natural relation to the power of collecting taxes; to that of regulating trade; to that of providing for the common defense."

"All of the specified powers of government are sovereign . . . the incorporation of a bank is a constitutional measure; and . . . the objections taken to the bill, in this respect, are ill-founded."

Convinced, Washington signed the bank bill on February 25, 1791. In doing so, he inadvertently made Jefferson and Madison Hamilton's political enemies from that point on.

∞

To give the Bank of the United States as broad an ownership as possible, Hamilton set the sale price of shares at $25 each. He also limited the number of votes shareowners could have so that no individual or corporation could gain control of the bank.

When Madison learned the bank shares were to go on sale in Philadelphia in April 1791, he objected. "Those living any distance from Philadelphia will not have a fair opportunity to buy shares," he said.

Hamilton promptly established a new date: the Fourth of July. When the bank doors opened in Philadelphia on that historic date, prospective buyers "rushed in like a torrent," one newspaper said. "If a golden mountain had been kindled, emitting from its crater a lava of the purest gold, the crowd would not have been greater, or exhibited more intense eagerness to share in the plunder."

In two hours, the 4,000 shares available to the public were oversubscribed. The bank stock was also oversubscribed when it went on sale in Boston and New York the same day. Among the subscribers were several states, Harvard College, and thirty members of Congress.

The sale of the bank stock set off a wild wave of speculation. By August, the $25 certificates were selling for $325.

The sale, however, had a side effect that Hamilton had not anticipated. Since farmers in the south had little cash to invest and were wary of banks, the principal owners of the Bank of the United States were mostly in the north.

And while the bank provided a solution to the nation's financial problems, it also served to fur-

*Secretary of the Treasury Alexander Hamilton
(second from right) is pictured with other
Cabinet members and the president (from left):
Secretary of War Henry Knox, Secretary of
Foreign Affairs Thomas Jefferson, Attorney
General Edmund Randolph (with back turned),
and George Washington.*

ther divide the country politically. At the same time, however, Hamilton's influence and popularity soared. A college in upstate New York was named after him (it still exists); he became trustee of his alma mater, Columbia; Dartmouth College presented him with an honorary degree as Doctor of Laws and so did Harvard, with these words: "to the (man) whose wisdom and unremitted exertions these United States owe so much of their present tranquillity and prosperity, and the national respectability."

In addition, a portrait of Hamilton painted by John Trumbull was hung in New York's City Hall, and his figure was exhibited in Bowen's Wax Work museum near the New York Stock Exchange.

The accolades and expressions of prominence stemmed from a simple fact: The United States was enjoying an unprecedented wave of prosperity, which had been created mostly by the Constitution, but also by Hamilton's fiscal policies.

But all was not triumph for the brash and brilliant secretary of the treasury. To support his policies in Congress, he needed the votes of both Pennsylvania and his home state of New York.

In January 1791, Philip Schuyler, his father-in-law, and a major and powerful supporter, failed to be reelected to the New York state senate. With the help of Governor Clinton, New York's attorney general won the seat.

In reporting this turn of events to Hamilton, a friend wrote from Albany that the senator-elect was "avowedly your Enemy & stands pledged to his party for a reign of vindictive declamation against your measures."

The name of the new senator was Aaron Burr.

⚭

In early December 1791, Hamilton produced another lengthy and masterful paper titled "Report on the Subject of Manufacturers."

Written in response to a request made by Congress a year earlier, Hamilton argued that government should support industry for these reasons:

- It would strengthen the economics of agri culture.
- It would create jobs.
- It would attract immigrants.
- It would open opportunities for enterprise and investment.

At the outset of his report Hamilton made it clear that agriculture "has intrinsically a strong claim to preeminence over every other kind of industry" because it was "the immediate and chief source of subsistence [food] to man."

As Hamilton viewed the emergence of the United States, however, he saw a total dependence on agriculture as a danger. To survive and prosper, he insisted, the nation must also have a strong manufacturing base. If it did not, the bulk of the money made from agriculture would go to foreign countries for machinery and equipment for agriculture and for military purposes.

Hamilton was to say later that the United States (at that time) had two markets—one in the manufacturing north, the other in the agricultural south—and that both needed each other in order for the nation to grow and prosper.

He also noted that in a time when war was a common occurrence, a strong manufacturing base was needed to produce supplies for an army and navy so the nation could remain free and independent.

Hamilton's report clearly favored free competition and included recommendations on tariffs and government subsidies. In effect, it gave the country an economic blueprint for the future. And while it was not immediately adopted by Congress, it eventually—despite setbacks—established the United States as one of the most powerful and successful countries in the world.

In the 1790s, however, Hamilton's proposals created distrust and antagonism in many quarters, particularly in the south. A South Carolina planter, for example, opined that the Bank of the United States would gobble up the country, which one day would be known as "The United States of The Bank."

When Alexander Hamilton had argued for ratification of the Constitution before the New York state legislature, he said, ". . . we are attempting, by this Constitution, to abolish factions and to unite all parties for the general welfare."

Ironically, once Hamilton's policies were adopted, the new nation became sharply divided politically. By 1790, those who opposed his policies first called themselves "Republican Democrats," then "Republicans." And the head of this party—mostly behind the scenes—was Thomas Jefferson. His chief lieutenant was James Madison.

Those who defended Hamilton's policies, including the president, remained Federalists. But since Washington stayed aloof from political disputes and clung to the ideal of doing what was right, the leader of the Federalists was, unquestionably, Alexander Hamilton.

Thus, "The Little Lion," as Hamilton was often called, became the target of bitter partisan attacks. The Republicans, for example, accused him of leading a "corrupt squadron" that convinced the "legislature to legislate for their own interests in opposition to those of the people."

In their zeal to get rid of Hamilton, the Republicans (who were no relation to today's Republicans) constantly searched for evidence of wrongdoing—the kind of evidence that would force Hamilton to resign.

Late in 1792, as the second national election loomed, two prisoners in a Philadelphia jail said they had enough information about Hamilton's illegal speculation in government securities "to hang him."

When three eager Republicans got together and investigated, however, they found to their chagrin that Hamilton was not guilty of speculation, but of something else.

∽

The three congressmen—Frederick Muhlenberg, James Monroe, and Abraham Venable—suddenly appeared at Hamilton's office on a snowy morning in mid-December 1792 and said they wanted to ask him a few questions about his relations with one James Reynolds.

Reynolds, they said, claimed Hamilton was speculating in government securities, which, they emphasized, was "a crime."

When Hamilton was shown a letter that he had written to Reynolds, he noted that it made no mention of dealing in securities. But he admitted that he did know Reynolds.

Hamilton then made a mysterious offer: He would tell the congressmen all about his relationship with Reynolds but apparently only on the condition that they would never disclose what he revealed if he could prove his connection with Reynolds had nothing to do with his official duties as secretary of the treasury.

The congressmen, it seems, accepted Hamilton's terms and agreed to be at his home that evening to hear his story.

When the three congressmen arrived, Hamilton ushered them into a back room of his home. He explained that Betsey and the children were visiting friends in the country. He also noted that his assistant, Oliver Wolcott, would be present to witness the interview.

Without preliminaries, Hamilton said that he had been blackmailed by James Reynolds and Reynolds's wife, Maria, and had the documents to prove it. Maria Reynolds, he said sheepishly, was a young and exceptionally beautiful woman. She had arrived at Hamilton's office about a year earlier and asked for his help.

According to Hamilton, she said she had to come to Philadelphia from New York to find her husband, who had abandoned her. After finding her husband, she said Reynolds had been very cruel to her and left her again. Since Hamilton was from New York, she asked if he couldn't advance her enough money to return to her friends.

Hamilton said he told Mrs. Reynolds that he didn't have the money at the time, but that he could bring it to her house that evening. During the course of his visit, he said, Maria led him to her bedroom.

Hamilton said he received a letter from James Reynolds a few days later accusing him of breaking up the Reynolds' marriage. In the letter, which Hamilton showed the congressmen, Reynolds said, "You took advantage of a poor Broken harted women. You have acted in the part of the most Cruelest man in existence. She says there is no other man that she Cares for in this world. Now Sir you have been the cause of this Cooling of her affection for me."

Hamilton said Reynolds demanded one thousand dollars of Hamilton to assuage his feelings. Hamilton then admitted he paid Reynolds in two installments.

Hamilton said that as the affair with Maria went on, it became clear that Reynolds and his wife were working together to bilk him.

Reynolds not only demanded more money, but insisted that Hamilton give him a job in the treasury department. Hamilton said he refused to do so, even though Reynolds threatened to reveal all to Betsey.

To back up his story, Hamilton showed the congressmen several letters he had received from the blackmailers. In one, Maria threatened to commit suicide and begged him not to break off their relationship when he tried to do so.

"Oh, Col. Hamilton, what have I done that you should thus Neglect me?" she asked. "Let me beg of you to come and if you never see me again or if you think it best I will submit to it and take a long and last adieu. For heaven's sake keep me not in Suspense. Let me know your intentions."

Maria, Hamilton admitted ruefully, was a convincing actress. He also pointed out that Reynolds was in jail with an accomplice because the two had attempted to swindle former soldiers and officers of the Continental army. When this was discovered, it was Hamilton's assistant, Wolcott, who swore out the arrest warrants for the pair.

Obviously, Reynolds hoped the Republicans would get him out of jail if he gave them enough evidence to force Hamilton to resign.

Convinced that Hamilton was innocent of misconduct in office, the congressmen dropped their probe. Temporarily, at least, they also kept Hamilton's affair with Maria Reynolds to themselves. In doing so, they probably saved both Hamilton's career and his marriage.

To Hamilton's anger and disgust, the Republicans soon launched a public attack to force him from office.

This time, Hamilton was accused of having "juggled" the books after obtaining two loans from Europe that totaled $12 million. By January 1792, the Republicans were able to muster enough votes in the House of Representatives to launch an investigation based on charges that Hamilton had concealed shortages in the government's accounts, favored the Bank of the United States, and used loans to benefit speculators.

A committee of fifteen, headed by William B. Giles of Virginia, held hearings for several weeks. During these hearings more accusations were added, ranging from "violating the law and the Constitution" to "insulting Congress by issuing misleading reports" and "disregarding the public interest."

As Hamilton suspected, many of these charges were secretly slipped to Giles by Jefferson and abetted by Madison. The Republicans hoped that Hamilton would not be able to respond to their attack before Congress adjourned in early March, giving the public a long time to think about the allegations.

But Hamilton was determined to clear himself. With a handful of clerks and five assistants, he worked night and day for sixteen days to develop a complete and detailed history of his department's activities, which included not only the

This portrait, painted in 1792, was made during the time that Hamilton's work was being investigated by a committee that was fed information by his rivals Madison and Jefferson.

bank's records, but Hamilton's personal records and correspondence.

On February 27, only three days before the session was to end, Giles put nine resolutions to a vote. All were soundly rejected.

❧

As Washington's first term as president drew to a close, Hamilton's feud with Jefferson and Madison escalated rapidly. Hamilton discovered that the two had persuaded Philip Freneau, a New York writer dubbed "the Poet of the Revolution," to move to Philadelphia and start a newspaper to support their views. He also learned that Freneau was given a job in Jefferson's foreign affairs department as part of his compensation.

When Freneau's new paper opened fire on Hamilton, Hamilton complained to the president. He said that Jefferson, by opposing the administration's policies, "had sown the seeds of discord in the Executive branch of the government in the infancy of its existence."

And while he favored freedom of the press, Hamilton said that it was wrong for a member of the president's cabinet to pay someone to attack the administration policies—policies that Jefferson should have supported.

For his part, Jefferson pointed out that the editor of another newspaper received advertising from the treasury department and had often praised Hamilton. Jefferson also complained that Hamilton had become so powerful that he was taking over the executive department. He also warned the president to beware of Hamilton's efforts to create a change "in the present form of republican government to that of a monarchy, of which the English Constitution is the model."

Deeply disturbed by the rivalry, Washington wrote to both men. To Jefferson, he said, "How unfortunate and how much it is to be regretted, that whilst we are encompassed on all sides with avowed enemies and insidious friends, that internal dissension should be harrowing and tearing at our vitals. The last, to me, is the most serious, the most alarming, and the most afflicting of the two."

Washington used different words in his letter to Hamilton, but the ideas were the same. While the mudslinging between the two secretaries moderated, one thing was now certain. The torrent of publicity generated by the feud established that there were now two clearly defined political parties in the United States: Hamilton headed one, the Federalists; and Jefferson headed the other, the Republicans.

The warring secretaries agreed that Washington should remain in office for a second term, but predictably, they differed on their choice for vice president.

While the Federalists named John Adams as their candidate, the Republicans at first got behind Governor Clinton of New York, an avowed anti-Federalist.

Since Hamilton gave the Federalists the slogan "Unanimity and Exertion," he put his personal feelings aside and applauded Adams, saying the

New Englander was "a real friend to genuine liberty, order and stable government."

But Hamilton became alarmed when Rufus King, a New York senator and one of his closest allies, reported that the Republicans might not stick with Governor Clinton for vice president. "Aaron Burr is industrious in his canvass for the Vice Presidency," King said.

Burr for vice president instead of Clinton? Did Burr have enough support from Jefferson to win?

Since Hamilton and Burr had crossed paths many times, he knew that Burr was the kind of man who was loyal to no one but himself. Nevertheless, Hamilton was taking no chances. In letters to several of his followers he characterized Burr as "a corrupt individual for or against nothing, but as it suits his interest or ambition" and "a bold, enterprising and intriguing opportunist."

"In a word," he added, "if we have an embryo Caesar in the United States, it is Burr!"

Washington was reelected unanimously. Adams was reelected with 77 votes. Burr got one vote.

But the 1792 election did not end the Hamilton-Burr rivalry.

Hamilton soon tangled with Jefferson over another issue: power.

How much power did the president of the United States have under the six-year-old Constitution? Enough to declare war? Enough to enact foreign policy without the blessing of Congress?

These and other serious questions confronted the Washington administration early in 1793 after French revolutionaries executed King Louis XVI and other royals, and declared war against England, Spain, and Holland. These questions also sparked another bitter clash between Hamilton and Jefferson and their respective followers, for this reason: The United States had signed a treaty of alliance with France during the American Revolution. Under its terms, the United States was to aid France if that country was attacked, primarily by protecting its territories in the West Indies.

The United States was also obliged to allow French vessels to bring cargo into American ports and take on supplies.

Hamilton pointed out that the treaty put the United States in the position of favoring France over England, the nation's most important trading partner.

Supporting the French, he insisted, could lead to war. As a result, he suggested that the United States suspend the treaty of alliance.

Jefferson disagreed. He pointed out that the French government was sending an envoy named Edmond Genet to the United States to improve relations between the two countries. He said the envoy should be courteously received and the terms of the treaty with France honored. On that point, the president sided with Jefferson.

Hamilton then suggested that the president issue a proclamation declaring that the United States was a neutral country and did not favor one side or the other.

Jefferson objected. Congress was not in session and he argued that the Constitution did not give the president the power to issue such a proclamation.

Washington now agreed with Hamilton. He signed a proclamation declaring that the United States would not take sides in the war between England and France, but would be "friendly and impartial."

The proclamation, however, raised two questions: Could the United States remain neutral? And since France had helped America achieve its independence, would the public support the president's decision?

When Edmond Genet landed in Charleston, South Carolina, in the spring of 1793 and leisurely made his way overland to Philadelphia, the Americans he encountered made it clear that they had not forgotten the role France played in the American Revolution.

"I live in the midst of continual parties," he said not long after his arrival in the capital. "Old Man Washington is jealous of my success, and of the enthusiasm with which the whole town flocks to my house."

Jefferson seemed oblivious to Genet's arrogance. "He offers everything and asks nothing," Jefferson said.

But Jefferson was wrong. There *was* something Genet wanted: money. When Genet asked that payments on money owed France be speeded up, Hamilton balked, and with good reason. He knew that Genet hoped to raise an army of Americans to attack the Spanish settlements in Florida and New Orleans, and these attacks could lead to war with Spain.

He also knew that Genet had already enlisted American privateers (privately owned ships) to capture British ships and, when they were successful, to bring them into American ports, where their cargoes were sold.

Genet's activities brought a howl of protest from the British government. Jefferson's response was that British ships captured by the French belonged to the French. And because of the treaty with France, he also insisted that ships commissioned by Genet could operate from U.S. ports.

Hamilton again asserted that Jefferson's position could lead to war. Washington agreed. He ruled that French privateers could no longer be outfitted in U.S. ports or enter them.

Genet ignored Washington's orders. When the French captured a fast brigantine named *Little Sarah*, Genet ordered it brought to Philadelphia and—right under the government's nose—proceeded to have it armed.

Early in July, Jefferson told Genet that *Little Sarah* should not sail until the matter was discussed with the president, who was at Mount Vernon but would soon return.

A defiant Genet said he planned to move *Little Sarah* downriver so the refitting could be speeded up. Then he warned, "Let me beseech you not to permit any attempt to put men on board of her.

She is filled with high-spirited patriots, and they will resist."

An alarmed Jefferson promptly met with Hamilton, Pennsylvania Governor Thomas Mifflin, and Secretary of War Henry Knox to discuss the situation. Hamilton said *Little Sarah* should not be permitted to sail. If necessary, he said, the ship should be sunk by shore batteries if it tried to leave.

This, Jefferson said, could lead to war with France.

And if *Little Sarah* sailed, Hamilton responded, it could mean war with England.

While the two argued, *Little Sarah* put to sea with a new name, *La Petite Democrate* (*The Little Democrat*).

Genet was soon replaced. The threat of war with England was averted, but not for long.

The end of 1793 brought another clash between Hamilton and his Republican rivals.

Jefferson resigned as secretary of foreign affairs and returned to his plantation at Monticello. This seemed to put James Madison at the helm of the Republicans.

In January 1794, Madison urged the government to adopt seven "Commercial Propositions" aimed at crippling commerce with England. His proposals, he said, would be a boon to the American economy because it would free the nation from "the caprice, the passions, the mistaken calculations of interest, the bankruptcies and the wars of a single foreign country."

Hamilton called Madison's plans an effort "to cultivate the connection and intercourse with the French nation." If adopted, he warned, they could provoke a war with England.

He also pointed out that Americans would be hurting themselves by curbing commerce with England. The United States, he said, had imported $14 million in goods from Britain the previous year, but only $150,000 worth from France. In addition, seventy-five percent of the nation's exports went to England.

Hamilton, however, was losing his argument with the Republicans because in the Mediterranean Sea Barbary pirates, believed to be controlled by England, were seizing American ships and cargoes and killing and torturing American seamen. Furthermore, Britain's governor-general of Canada was believed to have put the Indians of the northwest on the warpath against American frontiersmen.

Reflecting a sudden wave of hatred that swept the country, one American said, "Our blood is in flame! Yea we are ready to curse the hard-hearted Pharaoh who sits on the British throne."

At the same time, Hamilton asked Congress to build a navy, strengthen harbors, and create a continental army of 25,000 and state militias that would total 80,000.

He also suggested that someone should go to London and try to work out a settlement of grievances with the British. A group of Federalist senators agreed, and in March 1794 asked Washington to send Hamilton to England because he possessed "talents of the first order" and enjoyed "the confidence of the friends of Peace and of the government and whose character was unexceptionable in England."

The Republicans, in various forms, roared their protest. Washington, fully aware of the controversy aroused by the recommendation, appointed Chief Justice John Jay for the assignment.

Hamilton was delighted. He wrote Betsey, who was in Albany, "there is every prospect" that America would no longer bow to French power.

The Republicans, however, were concerned that Jay, a Federalist, might give the British too much power over American affairs.

∞

While John Jay was opening discussions with the British government, Americans at home turned their attention to another issue: taxation. In one respect, the Americans of yesterday were no different from those of today; they hated to pay federal taxes.

In 1791, the target of much displeasure was Alexander Hamilton, the man who drafted a set of internal tax laws (excise taxes) and convinced Congress to pass them. These taxes were imposed on a wide variety of American-made items, including snuff (pulverized tobacco), sugar, carriages, and alcoholic beverages.

The revenue was needed, Hamilton argued, to help pay the government's expenses, in particular those incurred in building up the army and a navy.

But those affected claimed that by taxing certain items, the law was "discriminatory." If

Hamilton wasn't stopped, it was argued, the government "would soon tax kisses between sweethearts."

Snuff manufacturers, who insisted that their product was "good for headaches and cleared the eyes," were so outraged that many threatened to leave the country. Southern planters were also provoked. The tax on carriages, they said, singled out the rich. "States which impose unequal taxes are masters, those which pay them are slaves," cried Virginian John Taylor in protest.

Another Virginian, Daniel Hylton, was so furious he decided to take the government to court on grounds that the tax on carriages was "unconstitutional." Taylor, a lawyer and Republican congressman, agreed to represent Hylton in court.

Hamilton warned that if the government lost the case, the nation's whole system of taxation would collapse and the country would be in serious trouble.

When the lower federal court rendered a split decision, Taylor told carriage owners they could ignore the tax. Alarmed, the government decided to bring the case before the Supreme Court. Its objective was to make it clear that the Constitution gave it the right to collect excise taxes.

When *Hylton* v. *United States* eventually came before the Court, Hamilton, representing the U.S. attorney general, demolished his opponent's argument that the carriage tax was a direct tax and as such violated the Constitution. The only direct taxes, Hamilton said, were poll taxes and taxes on land and buildings.

Hamilton, then thirty-nine, made a three-hour presentation that was described as "brilliant." In a ruling that stood for almost a century, the Court agreed with Hamilton.

On the western frontier, however, the excise tax sparked an armed rebellion among farmers when it was applied to one of their most important products: whiskey.

Because transporting grain over the Appalachian mountain range (to sell) was extremely difficult, farmers on the western frontier beyond the mountains converted it into whiskey. And because there was a scarcity of money available in the West, whiskey was often traded for a variety of goods.

When whiskey was taxed, those who made it howled in protest. Even if they wanted to pay the tax, the "Whiskey Boys" said they had no money to do so.

When Hamilton's agents visited local stills to collect taxes owed the government, there were armed confrontations, violence, and riots. Some agents were tarred and feathered.

After a mob of Whiskey Boys in western Pennsylvania threatened to attack Pittsburgh, President Washington told his Cabinet that the "most spirited and firm measures were necessary" to quell the disorders. "If such proceedings were tolerated there was an end to the Constitution," he added.

Since Congress was not in session and Secretary of War Henry Knox was away, the president obtained authority from the Supreme Court to call out militiamen from Pennsylvania, New Jersey, Maryland, and Virginia to put down the rebellion.

Donning their old uniforms, the president and Hamilton left Philadelphia on September 30, 1794, for Carlisle, Pennsylvania, where troops were to be organized and supplied.

When the army of about 12,000 men reached the eastern reaches of the mountains, Washington returned to the capital. He left Henry "Light Horse Harry" Lee in command, with Hamilton as his immediate subordinate.

Hamilton and Lee expected a fierce battle when they reached western Pennsylvania. But as the militiamen marched through village after village, all was peaceful and quiet.

Anxious to collar and punish the ringleaders of those who defied the United States government, the army rounded up about 150 suspects. Only two were indicted for treason. Both were eventually pardoned. The so-called Whiskey Rebellion was over.

Hamilton returned to Philadelphia on November 29. Three days later, he told the president he would resign on January 31, 1795, to return to his law practice so he could increase his income and properly take care of his large family.

Part VI

Two months after Hamilton resigned from the treasury, a copy of the treaty John Jay had worked out with the British arrived in America. When word of the terms leaked out, it touched off the biggest political battle yet in the new nation's history.

Because he had coached Jay before Jay's departure for England, Hamilton supported the treaty, which included agreement on the following principal points:

- The British promised to evacuate their military posts in the northwest by 1796.
- America's right to trade with the British West Indies was limited.
- The United States would pay its prewar debts to England.
- The British would pay for the illegal captures of American ships.

- Unsettled questions would be referred to comissions appointed by both sides.
- U.S. trade to Great Britain and India would be legalized.
- The United States agreed not to export several West Indian products.
- The United States agreed that privateers would not be outfitted in American ports and no captured cargoes would be brought into American ports and sold.

The Senate approved the treaty and sent it to the president for his signature. Almost immediately, however, it was bitterly assailed, especially in the seaport towns and by the Republicans, who felt that Jay had made too many concessions.

In Philadelphia, for example, a mob attacked the home of the British minister and John Jay was hanged in effigy and reviled as a traitor.

When Hamilton, who had moved back to New York, attended a lunch-hour outdoor meeting and tried to explain the terms of Jay's treaty to a crowd of mostly mechanics and laborers, he was stoned before he could utter a word.

Encouraged by the wave of opposition to "Jay's Treaty," Republicans in the House of Representatives tried to nullify it by denying funds to carry out its terms.

Convinced that this could only lead to war, Hamilton and New York Senator Rufus King launched a series of articles designed to turn the tide of public opinion in favor of the treaty.

In July 1795, Hamilton implied that the United States was still in its infancy and too weak to court a war. He went on to say that the purpose of Jay's mission to England had been "substantially obtained."

Jay's Treaty, he said, was "a reasonable one, as good a one as ought to have been expected; as good a one as there is any prospect of obtaining hereafter; one which is consistent with our honor to accept, and which our interest bids us to close with."

In all, there were thirty-eight essays. Signed "Camilius," most were written by Hamilton. The campaign was successful. In April 1796, after being flooded with mail favoring the treaty, the House voted 51 to 48 to support it.

The bitter battle, highlighted by the attacks of Republican newspapers and writers, however, persuaded Washington to leave office at the end of his second term. "I desire to be buffeted no longer in the public prints by a set of infamous scribblers," he said.

In his every spare moment from the middle of May 1796 to the end of July, Hamilton poured his energy into a public address he had been asked to write that embraced a vision of the future of the United States and argued that peace, security, and prosperity could only be achieved by a strong union.

And after each day's effort, he would call Betsey to his office and read what he had just written to "see how it sounded on the ear."

Among the passages he read aloud were these:

> The Unity of Government which
> constitutes you as one people, is
> also dear to you. It is justly so; for
> it is a main Pillar in the Edifice of
> your real independence; the support
> of your tranquillity at home, your
> peace abroad; of your safety, of
> your prosperity; of that very Liberty
> which you so highly prize....
>   With slight shades of difference,
> you have the same religion, man-
> ners, habits, and political principles.
> You have in a common cause
> fought and triumphed together.
> The Independence and Liberty you
> possess are the work of joint coun-
> cils and joint efforts—of common
> dangers, sufferings and successes.

The document warned of "geographical discrimi-
nations" and "small but artful and enterprising"
minorities.

"The basis of our political system is the right
of the people to make and to alter their Constitution of Government. But the Constitution
which at any time exists, 'till changed by an
explicit and authentic act of the whole people, is
sacredly obligatory to all."

To pay for Government debts, there must be
revenue; "to have revenue there must be taxes,"
he said, and added that "no taxes can be devised

which are not more or less inconvenient and unpleasant."

"Observe good faith and justice towards all nations. Cultivate peace and harmony with all." He warned, however, that the nation should be "constantly awake" against the "insidious wiles of foreign influence."

"The great rule of conduct for us, in regard to foreign nations," he went on, "is, in extending our commercial relations, to have with them as little political connection as possible."

Hamilton, however, was not the sole author of this historic document. Four years earlier, at the end of his first term, Washington had asked James Madison to help him prepare a farewell address, which, of course, he never used.

Near the end of his second term, Washington gave the original draft to Hamilton and asked him to revise it, or "throw the whole into a different form."

Historians agree that at least half of this now-famous farewell address was authored by Hamilton. They also agree that Washington and Hamilton shared the same vision of the times, tribulations, and future of America.

⚭

In the 1790s, there were sixteen states in the Union. In eight, the presidential electors were chosen by popular vote; in the remaining eight by state legislatures. Each elector, under the rules then in effect, was to cast two ballots. The candidate who received the highest number of votes would become president, and the one with the second highest number would be vice president.

The presidential election of 1796 may seem strange by today's standards. The leading candidates, John Adams (Federalist) and Thomas Jefferson (Republican), stayed home. The campaigns were run by party leaders in each state. The issues were fairly simple: A vote for Jefferson meant a vote for a stronger connection with France. A vote for Adams signaled closer ties with Great Britain.

The Republican party chiefs backed Jefferson as the candidate for president and Aaron Burr of New York, once again, as vice president. To drain away southern votes and keep Jefferson from winning the presidency, the Federalists put Thomas Pinckney of South Carolina on the ticket with John Adams.

Since Adams was not popular in the south and west, there existed a possibility that Pinckney would get more votes than Adams. But when the votes were counted, Adams became president with seventy-one votes, and Jefferson vice president with sixty-eight. Pinckney received fifty-eight votes and Burr thirty.

Although he won the presidency, Adams was convinced that Hamilton had worked against him in the belief that Pinckney would be elected president.

He was right. Hamilton saw Adams as too independent. Adams would never accept advice from Hamilton, but Pinckney would. Or so Hamilton believed.

Years later, Hamilton admitted he favored Pinckney because he thought Pinckney was the best man.

As for Adams, he was later to characterize Hamilton as "a proud, spirited, conceited, aspiring mortal" and also as the "bastard brat of a Scotch peddler."

Five and a half years after Hamilton's affair with Maria Reynolds had ended, his past came back to haunt him.

In the spring of 1797, an enemy of Hamilton's hired James T. Callender, an unethical writer, to produce a pamphlet titled "The History Of The United States for the year 1796," which included the charge that Hamilton and James Reynolds were involved in illegal speculative ventures.

To support the charge, Callender published some of the documents Hamilton had given the three congressmen who confronted him with the same charges in 1791.

Callender, who had been run out of England for writing libelous stories, said Hamilton's confession of his affair with Maria was simply a cover-up for his illegal activities.

Although the three congressmen issued statements absolving Hamilton of any wrongdoing insofar as his office was concerned, Hamilton unwisely decided to take his case to the public by publishing a ninety-five-page confession of the affair.

In this statement Hamilton said, "The charge against me is a connection to one James Reynolds of improper pecuniary speculation. My real crime is an amorous connection with his wife for a considerable time, with his privity and connivance, if not originally brought on by a combination between husband and wife with the design to extort money from me. . . . I can never cease to condemn myself for the pang which it may inflict in a bosom eminently entitled to all my fidelity and love," he added.

And while Betsey (who learned of his infidelity for the first time) forgave him, his enemies rejoiced and attacked him with glee.

Republican papers described him as a "lecher" and "a monster." Hamilton, one writer charged, had made his own home "the rendezvous of his whoredom, taking advantage of the absence of his wife and children to introduce a prostitute to those sacred abodes of conjugal and filial retirement, to gratify his wicked purposes."

Soon, however, the nation's attention turned away from Hamilton's personal indiscretions to something far more important.

In 1796, the French government, emboldened by victory on European battlefields, had ordered its navy to seize all ships carrying cargo to and from England. And, despite the neutral status of the United States, dozens of American ships were captured, their cargoes confiscated and sold.

President Adams promptly sent three envoys to France to negotiate a change in the harsh French regulations. After a long wait, French representatives advised the Americans that unless they were willing to give government officials

$25,000 and lend France $12,800,000, negotiations were over. The Americans left for home. "Declare war on France!" was the cry then often heard in the United States.

Hamilton advocated patience, a quick buildup of the army, and construction of several battleships. Congress authorized a call-up of troops. It also created a department of the navy and gave the go-ahead for the construction of several warships. But the international crisis wasn't over.

∞

When the act was finally passed to raise the new army, President Adams asked his Cabinet who should be named commander in chief.

Alexander Hamilton, came the immediate response from Thomas Pickering, secretary of foreign affairs.

Adams disagreed. He appointed George Washington. Washington reluctantly accepted on two conditions: that he did not have to take the field until absolutely necessary, and that he could pick his immediate subordinates.

When Adams agreed to these conditions, Washington quickly named Hamilton as his second in command. Adams balked. He thought the post should go to Henry Knox.

Washington wouldn't budge. It was either Hamilton or he would resign his new commission. But he gave Adams an explanation. "By some," Washington said, "he (Hamilton) is considered as an ambitious man, and therefore a dangerous one. That he is ambitious, I shall readily grant, but it is of that laudable kind which prompts a man to excel in whatever he takes in hand. He is enterprising, quick in his perceptions, and his judgment intuitively great; qualities essential to a military character. . . . His loss will be irreparable."

Adams gave in, but years later complained that he had been forced to appoint "the most restless, impatient, artful, indefatigable and unprincipled intriguer in the United States, if not in the world."

After considerable delay because of congressional interference, Generals Hamilton, Washington, and Pinckney (also selected by Washington) began to organize the army in November 1798. The first task was to go through hundreds of applications for officer commissions.

One of those interviewed was Aaron Burr, who had been recommended for the rank of general, even though his highest rank during the Revolution was only that of colonel.

In a private interview, Hamilton asked Burr—as he did all other applicants—whether he would loyally support Washington as commander in chief. "I despise Washington as a man of no talents who can't spell a sentence of common English," Burr answered.

Without hesitation, Hamilton rejected Burr.

By early 1799, the French sent word through diplomatic channels that they were eager to resume peaceful relations with the United States.

To the surprise of everyone, including his Cabinet and members of Congress, President

Adams sent the name of William Vans Murray to the Senate as his choice as minister to France.

Although several senators finally persuaded Adams to send a three-man delegation overseas, the move made one thing clear: The possibility of war with France had ended, and with it the need for a standing army, which was soon dismantled.

For Hamilton, it also meant a return to his law practice. Following the death of George Washington at the end of the year, however, Hamilton turned his attention to the presidential election of 1800. This election was full of bizarre twists and turns but, in the end, pitted Hamilton against Aaron Burr.

∞

During the spring of 1800, Hamilton made a swing through New England to say farewell to the troops he would no longer command. Without a doubt, it was something of a triumph for Hamilton. As one newspaper said, the soldiers who heard him speak were often in tears, "not merely on account of this last interview with their General, but by the impressive sentiments which fell from his lips, enforced by the most charming eloquence and pointed diction."

In his remarks, however, Hamilton was often critical of President Adams, primarily because Adams repeatedly refused to take advice from Hamilton on foreign affairs (especially regarding relations with England and France). When Hamilton's critical statements were reported to Adams, the president erupted in anger, referring to Hamilton as "a bastard," an "alien," and the leader of "a damned faction" of "British partisans" who were trying to incite the French to declare war on the United States.

And when someone suggested Hamilton should be president, Adams snapped, "Mr. Jefferson is an infinitely better man, a wiser one I'm sure; and if president, will act wisely. I know I would sooner be vice president under him, or even Minister Resident at the Hague than be indebted to such a being as Hamilton for the presidency."

Hamilton immediately asked Adams for an explanation, especially for Adams's reference to the alleged "British faction." When Adams refused to answer, Hamilton—against the advice of his closest advisers—sent a pamphlet to leaders of his party "concerning the Public Conduct and Character of John Adams."

While he did not deny that Adams was patriotic and a man of integrity with "talents of a certain kind," Hamilton said Adams "does not possess the talents, adapted to the administration of government, and that there is great and intrinsic defects in his character, which unfit him for the office" of president.

Hamilton also accused Adams of often displaying "disgusting egotism, distempered jealousy," and "ungovernable indiscretion of temper."

Despite his feelings, Hamilton wanted the Federalists to remain in power. "I have finally resolved not to advise the withholding from

[Adams] of a single vote," he said. He then indicated that he was among those who, while dissatisfied with the president, would equally support Adams "and Mr. [Charles Cotesworth] Pinckney, whom [we] prefer."

He went on to say that he refrained from "a decided opposition" to Adams in the interest of harmony among the Federalists, because the Union depended on them to preserve "order, tranquility, liberty, property" and the "security of every social and domestic blessing."

Somehow, Aaron Burr obtained a copy of Hamilton's pamphlet and released excerpts to the newspapers. That marked the beginning of the end of not only the Federalist Party, but of Hamilton's political career.

∞

Aaron Burr was said to have been a bright, attractive, but unruly child. He graduated with honors from the College of New Jersey (now Princeton University) when he was sixteen.

While slight of build and only 5 feet 6 inches (168 centimeters) tall, he had joined Benedict Arnold's harrowing march to Quebec in 1775 and served with distinction.

In the spring of 1776, he left Canada for New York, where he became a member of Washington's headquarters staff. But Burr and Washington did not like each other, and Burr soon left to become aide to General Israel Putnam.

After serving in the battle of Long Island, Burr was commissioned a lieutenant colonel. Later, he

Aaron Burr

joined the army at Valley Forge, fought at Monmouth Court House, and subsequently testified for General Lee during Lee's court-martial.

Burr, about the same age as Hamilton, left the army early in 1779, obtained a law degree, and opened a practice in New York City. A short time later, Alexander Hamilton opened his law office only a few doors away from Burr's.

Since there were only about thirty lawyers in the city at that time, Burr and Hamilton were in frequent contact with each other, sometimes acting as cocounsel on the same case.

After Republican Governor George Clinton appointed Burr attorney general of New York, Burr was elected to the U.S. Senate. Failing to be reelected, he won a seat in the state legislature. Again, he was unable to win reelection.

Then he turned all his energy into organizing the Republicans of New York City. The organization he built was so powerful it enabled the Republicans to gain control of the New York legislature during the state elections in April 1799.

In May, as the Republican party faced the presidential election of 1800, it became clear that New York's twelve electoral votes were needed for victory. And since Jefferson was the overwhelming choice for president, the party leaders decided that the forty-three-year-old Burr would be a suitable and politically important running mate as vice president.

As many Federalists feared, Hamilton's writings about Adams so badly divided the Federalist party that it lost the election (Adams received sixty-five votes and Pinckney, sixty-four).

When the Republican votes were tallied, Jefferson and Burr had each received seventy-three votes. As required by the Constitution, the tie threw the election into the House of Representatives. In doing so, it prompted Hamilton to once again flex his political muscles.

When Hamilton learned that many of the Federalist members of the House of Representatives would rather have Burr than Jefferson for president, he again went for his pen.

In one letter that best summed up his views about Burr, he said: "(Burr) has no principle, public or private; could be bound by no agreement; will listen to no monitor but his ambition."

He then suggested the Federalists vote for Jefferson, but wring from the candidate "assurances on certain points; maintenance of the present (economic) system, especially on the cardinal articles of public credit, a navy, neutrality."

But many of the Federalists, who had spent months tearing Jefferson down in favor of Adams, refused to suddenly embrace the Virginian. As a result, all voted for Burr, creating a deadlock over the presidency that held for thirty-five ballots. Before and during the voting, Hamilton was in correspondence with James A. Bayard, the lone delegate from tiny Delaware.

In one letter to Bayard, Hamilton struck the usual theme: "I could scarcely name a discreet man of either party in our State (New York), who does not think Mr. Burr the most unfit man in the United States for the office of President. Disgrace abroad, ruin at home, are the probable fruits of his elevation.

"For heaven's sake, my dear sir, exert yourself to the utmost to save our country from so great a calamity."

The thirty-sixth ballot took place on February 17, 1801. Bayard, who became convinced Jefferson would support some of the major Federalist policies, suddenly changed his vote. When he did, Thomas Jefferson became the nation's third president.

Early in 1801, Hamilton built a country house in upper Manhattan, which he named The Grange, after his family's ancestral home in Scotland. By then, Hamilton and Betsey had seven children and one more was on the way.

Their flock included Philip, Angelica, Alexander, James Alexander, John Church, William Stephen, and Eliza. The oldest and most promising was Philip, who showed a remarkable resemblance to his father.

The twenty-year-old Philip, who was well educated, seemed headed for a promising law career when he became involved in a dispute with another young lawyer named George Eacker while both were in a New York theater.

Several months before they met, Eacker, who was described as a "violent and bitter democrat,"

The Grange, located in upper Manhattan

had given a speech on the Fourth of July attacking Philip's father, the former secretary of the treasury.

While sitting in a theater box next to Eacker, young Hamilton and his friends began to berate him for the speech. Later, Eacker grabbed Philip Hamilton by the collar, shook him, and said, "I will not be insulted by a set of rascals."

More hot words led young Hamilton to challenge Eacker to a duel, even though he disapproved of dueling. Eacker eagerly accepted.

Since dueling was illegal in New York, the two young men and their seconds met on "the field of honor" (a place where a duel is fought) in Weehawken, New Jersey. Philip Hamilton was killed by a single shot.

The *New York Evening Post*, owned by his father and several friends, reported that Philip, "aware that the origin of the controversy lay with him, and averse to shedding blood, decided to reserve his fire, receive that of his antagonist and discharge his pistol in the air."

Alexander Hamilton, it was said, never fully recovered from this personal tragedy.

∞

Ironically, the fiscal policies Hamilton crafted for the United States and pushed through Congress enabled their once fiercest opponent, Thomas Jefferson, to buy the Louisiana Territory from the French in 1803 for about $15 million.

The purchase of this vast territory, however, alarmed Federalist extremists in New England headed by Thomas Pickering, former secretary of foreign affairs under George Washington.

Pickering feared that Jefferson planned to carve the Louisiana Territory into slave-holding states. And, under the law that permitted three-fifths of slave populations to be counted in elections to the House of Representatives, he saw "Negro Presidents and Negro Congresses" in America's future.

Pickering also envisioned the day when the New England states would lose not only political power, but population and industry as land-hungry New Englanders fled to the open west.

Pickering's solution to this imagined dilemma was to form a northern confederacy and secede from the Union. He realized, however, that the confederacy could not succeed unless New York joined its ranks, and so he looked to a prominent New Yorker to help: Alexander Hamilton.

Horrified by Pickering's grandiose plans, Hamilton turned him down. Pickering then approached Aaron Burr.

While Burr didn't openly commit himself to Pickering's proposal to join the northern confederacy, he eagerly accepted the offer by a group of Pickering supporters and unhappy Republicans that he run for governor of New York.

And, even though he narrowly missed being elected president as a Republican, he now identified himself as a Federalist. But where did that leave the Federalist party? Should it support Burr for governor of New York?

To answer these questions, the Federalist party held a meeting in Albany during the time Hamilton was working on a court case in Albany. Hamilton, fearful that the Federalists might decide to support Burr, made arrangements to attend.

As he anticipated, the discussion at the meeting turned to support of Burr. When given the floor, Hamilton repeated many of his critical comments about Burr. Now, however, he also warned that Burr, "a man of irregular and insatiable ambition," would very likely push for "dismemberment of the Union [by joining Pickering]."

He then startled the meeting by urging support of Morgan Lewis, the candidate of the opposition Republican party!

When the Federalist vote was counted, it was clear that Hamilton had been ignored. Virtually every Federalist in the state voted for Burr.

But Lewis was elected. And Burr suffered the worst defeat of any candidate for governor up to that time.

Burr's political career, it seemed, was over.

⚭

In April 1804, two months after Burr's ignominious defeat at the polls, an Albany newspaper reported that a Dr. Charles D. Cooper, while attending a dinner party, quoted Hamilton as saying he "looked upon Mr. Burr to be a dangerous man, and one who ought not be trusted with the reins of government."

"I could detail to you, a still more despicable opinion which General Hamilton has expressed of Mr. Burr," Cooper was said to have added.

On June 18, William Van Ness called on Hamilton at his office in New York, showed him the newspaper article, and gave him a note from Burr.

The note demanded that Hamilton respond to the article with "a prompt and unqualified acknowledgment or denial of any expression which would warrant the assertions of Dr. Cooper."

In his reply, Hamilton said, "'Tis evident that the phrase 'still more despicable' admits of infinite shades from very light to very dark. Between gentlemen, 'despicable and more despicable' are not worth the pains of distinction . . . I trust, on mature reflection, you will see the matter in the same light with me. If not, I can only regret the circumstances, and must abide by the consequences."

Burr was not happy with Hamilton's answer. For years, his political career had been frustrated by Hamilton. He was determined to have "satisfaction." And when Hamilton refused to yield, Burr challenged him to a duel.

Before the duel took place, Hamilton calmly drew up his will and wrote two letters to his wife, whom he sometimes called "Eliza."

In the first letter, dated July 10, 1804, Hamilton said, "This letter, my dear Eliza, will not be delivered to you unless I shall have first terminated my earthly career, to begin, as I humbly hope, from redeeming grace and divine mercy, a happy immortality. If it had been possible for me to have avoided the interview, my love for you and my precious children would have been alone a decisive motive."

He said, however, that he could not avoid the duel "without sacrifices which would have made me unworthy of your esteem." In closing, he said, "adieu, best of wives—best of women. Embrace all my darling children for me."

In the second letter, written at ten o'clock that night, Hamilton clearly indicated he would not fire at Burr. "The scruples of a Christian have determined me to expose my own life to an extent, rather than subject myself to the guilt of taking the life of another," he said. "But you had rather I should die innocent than live guilty. Heaven can preserve me, I humbly hope. God's will be done! The will of a merciful God must be good. Once more, Adieu, my darling, darling wife."

At dawn the next morning, accompanied by his second, Nathaniel Pendleton, and his personal physician, Hamilton was rowed across the Hudson River to Weehawken—to the very grounds where his son, Philip, had been killed.

Burr and his second were there waiting.

Very quickly, the two parties followed the formalities prescribed by the "code duello": lots were drawn to establish positions of the duelists, the second that was to give the commands was chosen, pistols were loaded and examined.

Then came the final instructions: "If one of the parties fires, and the other hath not fired, the opposite second shall say 'one, two, three, fire,' and he shall then fire or lose his shot. A snap or a flash is a fire."

The duelists moved ten paces apart. On the command "Present!" two shots were heard.

Burr's hit Hamilton in the stomach. Hamilton's went wild, his gun discharging when he fell.

When his physician reached him, Hamilton gasped, "Take care of that pistol; it is undischarged and still cocked; it may go off and do harm. Pendleton knows . . . I did not intend to fire at him." As the physician attended Hamilton, Burr and his second left.

This wood engraving is just one of the many views artists created of the tragic duel that took place on July 11, 1804.

Hamilton was taken back across the river to lower Manhattan and rushed to the home of William Bayard, a longtime friend.

Soon, Betsey and the children were at his side. As Betsey tried to comfort Hamilton, surgeons from a French frigate tied up in the harbor tried to save him. But Burr's bullet had blasted through Hamilton's liver and was lodged in his spine. There was nothing the doctors could do.

As he lingered in great pain, Hamilton asked to be accepted into the Episcopal Church and receive the sacrament. But because there was such a strong public feeling against dueling, the clergymen who were summoned to attend Hamilton refused his request.

Toward the end, a bishop named Moore was called. Convinced that Hamilton was opposed to dueling, Moore administered the sacrament.

Some thirty-six hours after he had been shot, America's bold, idealistic, and courageous Little Lion was dead. He was forty-seven years old.

≪ Epilogue ≫

In the months and years following the duel with Alexander Hamilton, Aaron Burr's life took several bizarre turns. Toward the end of his term as vice president, for example, he hatched a plot to take the western part of the United States out of the Union, establish New Orleans as its capital, and install himself as head of what would be a vast new country.

When the British refused to advance him half a million dollars and a navy, he sailed down the Mississippi with another proposal: He would "liberate" Mexico and East and West Florida from Spanish rule and take over as emperor.

When President Jefferson heard of Burr's scheme, he had him arrested and brought to trial in Richmond, Virginia, on a charge of treason. Acquitted, Burr went into exile in Europe, where he continued his wild schemes, one of which was to return Canada to the French. Strangely enough, the smooth-talking, debonair Burr attracted a large following wherever he went and seemed to have no trouble raising money.

Burr returned to the United States and his law practice in 1812 and, at seventy-seven, married a former prostitute, who was also a wealthy widow. When Burr began to squander her money on land speculation, his new wife left him after four months and filed for divorce. The divorce was granted the day Burr died, September 14, 1836.

Elizabeth Hamilton outlived Burr by several years and devoted all of her time and energy to taking care of her seven children and keeping her husband's name alive. She not only made a persistent effort to collect all his papers, letters, and journals, but tried repeatedly to have his biography published. Disappointed by several would-be authors, she finally turned to her son John C. Hamilton, who, after several years, produced a seven-volume edition covering his father's life. At the time, this was the most authoritative work about Alexander Hamilton and remained so for a century.

To ensure her husband's fame, Elizabeth Hamilton also campaigned for years to have the federal government buy and publish his papers. In August 1848, when she was ninety-one, Congress finally appropriated $26,000 to carry out her wishes. Ironically, Congress also authorized the same amount in the same bill for Jefferson's papers.

After her husband's death, Elizabeth Hamilton wore black clothes to indicate she was in mourning. She continued to wear black until she died in 1854 at the age of ninety-seven.

The writings of Betsey Hamilton (pictured here in her eighties) helped to keep her husband's name a prominent one in the history of the United States.

Hamilton's papers, so zealously collected and preserved by Elizabeth Hamilton and their son, James, clearly show that Hamilton, foreign-born to an unstable home, was one of the greatest American patriots and statesmen of his time. He played a key role in the American Revolution and a critical part in the creation and adoption of the Constitution. In addition, his visionary financial and economic plans not only saved the Union from ruin and dissolution after its birth, they set the young United States on a course that enabled it to become the most prosperous, powerful, and important nation in the world.

For these reasons, next to George Washington, Alexander Hamilton was arguably the nation's most important Founding Father.

∽ Important Dates ∽

1757 Alexander Hamilton is born on the island of
      Nevis on January 11
1772 Sails for America in October
1774 Enters Kings College on September 20
1776 Qualifies as New York's first artillery officer
1777 Becomes aide-de-camp to General George
      Washington at Morristown, New Jersey, on
      March 1
1780 Marries Elizabeth Schuyler on December 14
1781 Obtains a field command and moves to Yorktown,
      Virginia, with the main army on July 19
1782 First son, Philip, is born on January 22
1787 Arrives at the Constitutional Convention in
      Philadelphia on May 18, 1787, as a delegate from
      New York
      Writes and issues the first of the famous Federalist
      Papers on October 17
1789 Becomes first secretary of the treasury in
      September; issues famous report on public credit
      three months later
      Proposes establishment of a national bank on
      December 14
1791 President Washington signs the bank bill on
      February 25 after it was opposed by James
      Madison, Thomas Jefferson, and others
1793 A Republican attempt to drive Hamilton from
      office fails on February 27
1795 Resigns as secretary of the treasury on January
      31; in July, issues a series of thirty-eight essays
      supporting John Jay's treaty
1796 Works on Washington's farewell address from
      May to July
1797 Issues a lengthy pamphlet that contains a full con-
      fession of his affair with Maria Reynolds after it
      becomes publicly known in July
1804 Dies as the result of a gunshot wound received in
      a duel with political opponent Aaron Burr on
      July 11

∽ Bibliography ∽

Boatner, Mark Mayo III. *Encyclopedia of the American Revolution.* New York: David McKay, 1966.

Boorstin, Daniel J. *The Americans.* New York: Macmillan, 1965.

Brookhiser, Richard. *Alexander Hamilton: American.* New York: The Free Press, 1999.

Cook, Jacob Earnest. *Alexander Hamilton.* New York: Scribner, 1982.

Crouse, Anna Erskine and Russell Crouse. *Alexander Hamilton and Aaron Burr.* New York: Random House, 1958.

Flexner, James Thomas. *George Washington* (3 volumes). Boston: Little, Brown, 1967–1972.

Flexner, James Thomas. *The Young Hamilton: A Biography.* Boston: Little, Brown, 1978.

Gordon, John Steele. *Hamilton's Blessing: The Extraordinary Life and Times of Our National Debt.* New York: Walker and Company, 1997.

Higginbotham, Don. *The War of American Independence.* New York: Macmillan, 1971.

Johnson, Paul. *A History of the American People.* New York: HarperCollins, 1997.

Lodge, Henry Cabot. *Alexander Hamilton.* Broomall, PA: Chelsea House, 1969.

Miller, John C. *Alexander Hamilton: Portrait in Paradox.* New York: Harper & Brothers, 1958.

Miller, John C. *Sam Adams.* Boston: Little, Brown, 1936.

Morris, Richard B. *Alexander Hamilton and the Founding of the Nation.* New York: The Dial Press, 1957.

Morrison, Samuel Eliot. *The Oxford History of the American People.* New York: Oxford University Press, 1965.

Muzzey, David Saville. *Thomas Jefferson.* New York: Scribner, 1918.

Rogov, Arnold A. *Hamilton and Burr: A Fatal Friendship.* New York: Hill and Wang, 1998.

ꙮ Sources and Acknowledgments ꙮ

Thanks to the efforts of Elizabeth Hamilton, a great deal of material exists that is related to her husband's life and career, including his letters, essays, speeches, and court papers. The material for this work was based primarily on many of these important papers. Still, I owe a debt of gratitude to the many authors who went before me and sifted through the same material. Collectively, these authors provided me with insights and information I could not have obtained without reading their books.

Among the most helpful were: *Young Hamilton*, by James Thomas Flexner; *Alexander Hamilton—American*, by Richard Brookhiser; *Encyclopedia of the American Revolution*, by Mark Mayo Boatner III; *Alexander Hamilton—Portrait in Paradox*, by John C. Miller; *A History of the American People*, by Paul Johnson; *Alexander Hamilton and the Founding of the Nation*, by Richard B. Morris; *Washington*, (3 volumes) by James Thomas Flexner; *The Oxford History of the United States*, by Samuel Eliot Morrison; *The Historians History of the United States*, Volume I (several authors); *Thomas Jefferson*, by David Saville Muzzey; *Sam Adams*, by John C. Miller; *Hamilton And Burr—A Fatal Friendship*, by Arnold A. Rogov; *Hamilton's Blessing*, by John Steele Gordon; *Alexander Hamilton*, by Jacob Ernest Cook; and *Alexander Hamilton*, by Henry Cabot Lodge. The *Federalist Papers*, bound in a single volume, was also an important source of information.

Obviously most of these books were found in libraries. Those I visited most frequently are located in Philadelphia, Paoli, Exton, and Trydeffdrin, Pennsylvania. I want to thank the staffs at each of these libraries for their courtesy and assistance.

I must also thank Sara Landis for her helpful and constructive comments after reading the first draft of this book. Most of all, I am indebted to my editor at the Millbrook Press—Laura Walsh—for her intelligence, patience, and guidance throughout the life of this project.

❧ Index ❧

Hamilton, James (brother),
6–7
Hamilton, James (father),
5–6
Hamilton, John Church,
174, 184
Hamilton, Philip, 80–81, 87,
129, 174–176, 180
Hamilton, Rachel, 5–6
Hamilton, William Stephen,
174
Harpur, Robert, 16, 21
Harrison, Robert, 34
Henry, Patrick, 108, 110
Howe, Richard "Black Dick,"
23, 26
Howe, Sir William, 22, 27,
36–40, 48
Hylton, Daniel, 153

Jay, John, 36, 56, 108, 120,
152, 158, 159
Jefferson, Thomas, 120,
125–126, *127*, 131, 132,
134, 138, 142, 144–150,
163, 169, 173, 174, 176
Johnson, William Samuel,
102

King, Rufus, 146, 159
Knox, Henry, 22, 24, 28,
120, *134*, 150, 155,
166
Knox, Hugh, 12, 14

Lafayette, Marquis de, 38,
50, 52, *53*, 63, 65, 67,
72, 74, 76, 78
Lansing, John, Jr., 94, 99,
100, 102, 105
Laurens, John, 55, 56, 60,
61, 76, 82
Lavien, John Michael, 5, 6
Lavien, Peter, 5, 6
Learned, Ebenezer, 42, 44,
45

Lee, Charles, 20, 50–52,
54–55, 172
Lee, Henry "Light Horse
Harry," 155
Lee, Richard Henry, 108
Lewis, Morgan, 178
Lincoln, Benjamin, 73
Livingstone, Sarah, 61
Livingstone, William, 61
Louis XVI, King of France,
147

Madison, James, 84, 91, 98,
110, 115, 119, 122, *123*,
124–125, 128, 131–133,
138, 142, 150–151, 162
Martin, Luther, 104–105
Mason, George, 107
McHenry, John, 71
Mifflin, Thomas, 150
Monmouth Court House,
49–50, 52, *53*, 54, 172
Monroe, James, 138
Morris, Gouverneur, 102
Morris, Robert, 82–84
Muhlenberg, Frederick, 138
Murray, William Vans, 168

New Jersey Plan, 100
Newton, William, 10, 11

Paterson, William, 99–100
Pendleton, Nathaniel, 180,
181
Philadelphia, Pennsylvania,
27, 37, 38, 45, 48, *95*
Pickering, Thomas, 166,
176–178
Pinckney, Charles
Cotesworth, 170, 173
Pinckney, Thomas, 163, 167
Poor, Enoch, 42, 44, 45
presidential election
of 1792, 145–146
of 1796, 163
of 1800, 168, 172–174